Th  Anglia

Le D1465719 Centre

Keeping
and
Breeding
Amphibians

Keeping
and
Breeding
Amphibians

Caecilians, Newts, Salamanders,
Frogs and Toads

Chris Mattison

BLANDFORD

A BLANDFORD BOOK

First published in the UK 1993
by Blandford, a Cassell imprint
Villiers House, 41–47 Strand, London WC2N 5JE

Copyright © 1993 Chris Mattison

Reprinted 1994 (twice)

Distributed in the United States by Sterling Publishing Co., Inc.
387 Par Avenue South, New York, NY 10016-8810

Distributed in Australia by Capricorn Link (Australia) Pty Ltd
2/13 Carrington Road, Castle Hill, NSW 2154

Cataloguing-in-publication data for this title is available from
the British Library.

ISBN 0-7137-2328-9

Typeset by Litho Link Ltd, Welshpool, Powys, Wales

**Printed and bound in Slovenia
by printing house DELO – Tiskarna
by arrangement with KOROTAN ITALIANA**

Contents

Acknowledgements

As usual, it would not have been possible to write and illustrate a book of this scope without the help and co-operation of a large number of people who gave up their time to answer questions or allow their animals to be photographed. Although it is not feasible to name them all, the following have played a significant part in the project and I would like to extend my gratitude to them:

David Baker, Geoff Clarke, Jeremy Fletcher, Steve Halfpenny, Victor Kuilenburg (Dierenpark Ouwehand, Rhenen), Vicky Mattison, John Pickett, Terry Thatcher, Geoff Trinder, Paul Walker, Adam and April Wright (Coventry Reptiles).

Special thanks are due to Gretchen Davison who prepared the line drawings.

Editorial Note

METRIC CONVERSIONS

Throughout this book all measurements of temperature and length are given as metric.

Those readers who are more familiar with the Fahrenheit thermometer or the Imperial System of measurement might find the following formulae and conversion tables useful.

Temperature

To convert °C to °F:
$\times\ 9 \div 5 + 32$

°C		°F
10	=	50
15	=	59
20	=	68
25	=	77
30	=	86
35	=	95
40	=	104
45	=	113
50	=	122

Length

To convert cm to in:
$\div\ 2.54$

cm		in.
1	=	0.39
5	=	1.97
10	=	3.94
15	=	5.91
20	=	7.87
25	=	9.84
30	=	11.81
35	=	13.78
40	=	15.75
50	=	19.66
60	=	23.62
75	=	29.53
100 (1 m)	=	39.37 (3.3 ft)
200 (2 m)	=	78.74 (6.6 ft)
400 (4 m)	=	157.48 (13.1 ft)

Introduction

Keeping and breeding amphibians is one of the most specialized fields of animal husbandry. The word 'amphibian' comes from two Greek words: *amphi*, meaning 'both', and *bios*, meaning 'life'. Thus, amphibians are animals which live two lives, one in the water (as larvae, or tadpoles) and one on the land (as adults). In fact there are amphibians which skip the aquatic phase altogether and there are others which never leave the water even after they have metamorphosed into adults. The general idea, however, remains valid, and so those who intend to keep and breed amphibians must make themselves adept at maintaining small, delicate, aquatic creatures as well as slightly larger, slightly less delicate, terrestrial ones. He or she must combine the skill of the aquarist with that of the herpetoculturalist (and, possibly, with that of the horticulturalist as well) if his or her animals are to thrive.

The class Amphibia can be subdivided into three orders:

Caecilians (Apoda)	160 species
Newts and salamanders (Urodela)	360 species
Frogs and toads (Anura)	3500 species

This produces a total of about 4000 species. Not all of these are suitable for life in captivity; indeed, only a very small proportion are interesting enough, common enough and easy enough to care for to have made their way into the hobby. Other species may prove to be suitable and, as time goes on, some of these will also be introduced to the herpetoculturalist. In the meantine it is necessary to be aware of some basic principles, as well as some specific data, before amphibian keeping can be attempted.

The first eight chapters of this book deal with 'universal' principles:

information which can be applied to amphibians in general or to large groups of species. These chapters should be studied carefully because much of the information they contain is not repeated elsewhere: it is assumed that a basic understanding of the principles will have been grasped before specific details are looked up.

The remaining chapters deal with individual families, genera and species of amphibians. These accounts are by no means comprehensive. An attempt has been made to cover all the species most likely to appear in the pet trade, but new ones will undoubtedly appear from time to time. For these it is hoped that it will be possible to extrapolate from the information given for closely related species, or for species which hail from a similar habitat, and to arrive at a reasonably satisfactory captive environment.

The keeping of any animal must be undertaken only after careful consideration, and amphibians are no exception. Caring for them properly can be time-consuming and expensive – often the cost of the cages and equipment necessary far exceeds that of the animals themselves. Unless this is understood, it may be as well to look to less demanding animals for enjoyment.

It must also be understood that the science of keeping and breeding amphibians is in its infancy. Even where species have been bred regularly and on a relatively large scale, there is still much to learn. In particular, we know almost nothing about the diseases which affect amphibians. Neither do we know the optimum environmental parameters under which many of them should be kept – one often feels that they survive despite our efforts rather than because of them. The information given should therefore be regarded merely as a starting point, or a series of suggestions, rather than the last word in amphibian husbandry.

Finally it should be realized that many species are under threat in the wild and, although the pet trade contributes little or nothing to this state of affairs compared with habitat destruction and pollution, an irresponsible attitude will condemn future hobbyists to increased restrictions. Ideally all amphibians in the pet trade should be produced in captivity, so eliminating the need to replenish stocks from the wild. There seems to be little chance that this will be achieved in the near future, but it should be the aim of everyone keeping these animals to attempt to breed from them.

PART I

General Principles

CHAPTER 1

Background Biology

Amphibians are an enormously diverse group of vertebrates. Broadly speaking, they are small vertebrates with smooth, moist skins. They usually lay their eggs in water or in moist surroundings and the eggs hatch into aquatic larvae which feed and grow for a while until they metamorphose into small versions of their parents. There are, however, exceptions to all these statements and it is this diversity which makes amphibians so interesting, both to the zoologist and to the herpeto-culturalist.

As is well known, amphibians were the first vertebrate animals to move out of an aquatic environment and dwell on the land. This important event took place about 360 million years ago and made possible the evolution of more advanced groups – the reptiles, birds and mammals. The early amphibians suffered from the same draw-backs which limit the lives of most of their modern descendants. They never became completely independent of water because of the need to return to it occasionally in order to reproduce. Furthermore, their lungs are poorly developed and this necessitates a system for breathing over the entire surface of their skin (cutaneous respiration). In order for this to operate effectively the skin needs to be kept moist by secreting mucus from glands just beneath its surface, which gives amphibians their characteristic 'sliminess'. In a dry atmosphere, evaporation causes a continuous loss of this moisture and so, unless they are able to replenish it frequently, they rapidly dehydrate. Amphibians are therefore restricted to wet, damp or humid environments, such as freshwater swamps, the edges of ponds and streams or damp places underground, among leaf-litter or in rainforests.

A few modern amphibians have, to some extent, broken their link with water and have adapted to more arid environments by means of behavioural and structural modifications. Some of these species spend a large part of their life cocooned in underground chambers awaiting

1. Frogspawn in a suburban pond. Most amphibians are still tied to the water by virtue of the aquatic stages of their life-cycle.

spasmodic rainfall to release them temporarily in order to reproduce. Species such as these would obviously require specialized techniques if they are to breed in captivity. By and large, however, amphibians should be treated as animals which require a more or less moist substrate and/or a humid atmosphere if they are to thrive.

SIZE

The largest amphibians are the giant salamanders, *Andrias japonicus* from Japan and *A. davidianus* from China. These are aquatic salamanders which metamorphose but rarely, if ever, leave the water. They can grow to 1.5 m in length but, since they are both endangered, they are unlikely to be encountered in captivity. Another acquatic species, *Amphiuma tridactylum*, from North America, may grow to almost 1 m in total length but is slender and eel-like in build. Of the terrestrial salamanders, the Olympic salamander, *Dicamptodon ensatus*, from North America, and the European fire salamander, can both reach almost 30 cm in length, which probably makes them the largest.

Among the frogs, the Goliath frog, from West Africa, is usually regarded as the largest, at a total length of 30 cm. A couple of South American toads, *Bufo blombergi* and *B. paracnemis*, grow to over 20 cm in length, while of the more familiar species, the North American bullfrog, *Rana cateseiana*, and Colorado River toad, *Bufo alvarius*, and the South American marine (or cane) toad, *Bufo marinus*, all grow to about 15 cm.

Generally speaking, however, amphibians are small creatures, with salamanders being typically less than 20 cm long and relatively slender, whereas frogs and toads are more rotund but rarely exceed 10 cm in length.

COLOUR

The colours and markings which make amphibians so appealing to us are actually important factors in their struggle for survival. Most species are camouflaged in order to escape the attentions of predators, of which they have many. Such species are predominantly brown if they live in leaf-litter, green if they live in grass or bushes, and so on. Other species, though, may be brilliantly coloured, with patches of red, blue, orange and yellow, and these are usually advertising the fact they produce dangerously poisonous substances: the markings of the European fire salamander and the South American poison-dart frogs are excellent examples of this 'warning' coloration.

2. One of the largest amphibians which is likely to come the way of hobbyists is the cane toad, *Bufo marinus*.

3. The majority of amphibians are camouflaged, but few are as well protected as the Asian horned toad, *Megophrys nasuta* (see also photographs 55 and 83).

4. Some species, on the other hand, are anything but camouflaged! This astonishing creature is the blue poison-dart frog, *Dendrobates azureus*.

WATER BALANCE

In the matter of water balance, amphibians are faced with a dilemma. In order to breathe through their skin they must keep it moist. Their adaptations to a terrestrial lifestyle, therefore, are limited by the amount of evaporation which takes place and the dangers of dehydration. The way they get around these problems varies according to the species and its preferred habitat. Species which are aquatic or partially aquatic can easily replenish the water they lose through evaporation. Species living in more arid environments have thicker skins and rely less on cutaneous respiration. Desert-dwelling species have the capacity to burrow into the ground and form a thick, cocoon-like covering, consisting of several layers of skin, which protects them from dehydration and which is shed when the ground becomes damp again through rain.

In addition, species which are subjected to dry conditions for long periods of time have the ability to withstand a greater degree of dehydration than other vertebrates: spadefoot toads, for example, can lose nearly one half of their body weight through dehydration and still survive. They can replace lost water rapidly by absorbing it through the skin, by extracting it from their food or by drinking: if a dehydrated toad is placed in shallow water, its body weight will quickly return to normal.

No species of amphibian is able to survive in sea water, but a few species live in the brackish water of river estuaries and others, such as the European natterjack toad, *Bufo calamita*, are able to tolerate temporary salinity resulting from salt spray, for instance. In captivity, however, all amphibians should be kept in fresh water of the correct chemical type (see Chapter 3).

TEMPERATURE REGULATION

Amphibians are unable to control their body temperature from within. They are therefore at the mercy of the elements, which is why the majority of species live in warm climates. They are, however, able to function at lower temperatures than reptiles, for example, and a few species may remain active below freezing point. As a rule amphibians are forced to operate at the prevailing temperature of the habitat in which they live. They are able to lower their body temperature a little by panting, but their main defence against overheating is to hide in the shade or to burrow. When temperatures become critically low they may also burrow to escape from lethal extremes and this may be

5.   Amphibian skin is always moist: this allows gaseous exchange to take place over most of the animal's surface.

extended into a period of hibernation for species from cooler parts of the world.

The implications for captive amphibians are that their quarters must be heated or cooled to an appropriate temperature. The value of this will depend on their origin and, although they are able to tolerate an 'incorrect' temperature for a limited time, they will not thrive unless due attention is paid to the heating system of the cage (see Chapter 3).

FEEDING BIOLOGY

With a single exception (a Central American tree frog), all non-larval amphibians are predatory. As a rule they eat insects and other small invertebrates such as spiders, worms and slugs, but some of the larger species will tackle vertebrate prey such as rodents, young lizards and snakes and, very often, smaller amphibians. Furthermore, very few will eat prey which is not moving. This has very important implications for their care in captivity as an adequate supply of living food must be continuously available.

REPRODUCTIVE BIOLOGY AND LIFE-CYCLES

It is in the field of reproduction that amphibian evolution seems to have run riot. A large number of species have departed from the typical 'egg-tadpole-froglet' life-cycle altogether and have explored various evolutionary side roads. Since many of the more unusual – even bizarre – modes of reproduction are limited to species which are rarely seen in captivity, there is, unfortunately, no justification for a full account here. Several fascinating life histories can be found among some of the more frequently kept species, however, and these are often excellent choices for the vivarium.

Briefly, there appears to have been an evolutionary trend in amphibians towards reducing their dependence on water. By so doing they have been able to open up new possibilities in terms of habitats – steep hillsides, forest canopies and so on – and, at the same time, to reduce predation at the vulnerable, larval stage of the life-cycle. The trend has taken many forms and may involve one or other of the parents carrying the eggs, or the larvae, for all or part of their development. Other species lay large, terrestrial eggs, well-stocked with yolk, where the development takes place entirely within a tough outer membrane, the young animals breaking out only when they are fully developed. In extreme cases the eggs may be retained inside the body of the female and the young born fully formed.

LONGEVITY

The natural life-span of free-living amphibians is a subject about which we know very little. This is due, at least in part, to the lack of any useful techniques for marking young individuals so that they can be recognized if they are recaptured later in their life. Records for captive amphibians show that many species will live for fifteen years or more and some will exceed twenty. Species which tend to live to a ripe old age include the toads belonging to the genera *Bufo* and *Ceratophrys* and salamanders of the genera *Ambystoma* and *Salamandra*. Not all of the longevity records belong to robust species such as these, however, as there are records of tiny poison-dart frogs, genus *Dendrobates*, reaching fifteen years of age.

CHAPTER 2

Accommodation: Cages and Equipment

In keeping with the wide variety of amphibians, it follows that there is also a wide range of possibilities in terms of cages. Generally speaking, the choice of materials is between glass and plastic, but there will be variation in the actual design according to the species to be kept (and how many individuals) and whether the cage is to be on display or is merely a housing or breeding unit.

Plastic containers which can be pressed into use include clear or opaque food containers as well as purpose-made plastic aquaria and animal cages. Plastic is light, inexpensive and easily washed. Its main drawback is the difficulty with which it can be worked, and so plastic cages tend to be used only where a suitable size and design already exists. In addition it may become brittle and discoloured with age.

In practice amphibian keepers often use plastic boxes and bins for housing stock in quarantine, for large numbers of animals which are being maintained temporarily, for large batches of tadpoles and froglets or for animals which need individual housing for some reason or another. The containers range in size from small lunch boxes with a capacity of less than 1 litre to large plastic tubs or bins holding several hundred litres. Inflatable plastic containers, such as children's paddling pools, may also be pressed into use occasionally, especially where a shortage of space needs to be overcome temporarily, as they can be stored away conveniently when not in use.

Glass cages can be self-built or bought ready-made. Ready-made designs are usually rectangular in shape, based as they are on the traditional aquarium. These cages, or fish-tanks, are ideal for keeping aquatic amphibians, such as axolotls, clawed frogs and so on, and require no modification other than the fitting of an escape-proof lid. All-glass tanks made with silicone aquarium sealer are preferable to those made using the more traditional method of glazing a frame made of angle iron. These tanks will last indefinitely provided they are not

6. Simple accommodation in the form of a plastic food container, a piece of foam rubber and a centimetre or two of water is all that is required for a number of amphibian species. This type of housing is ideal for animals which are in quarantine or which are kept purely as breeding stock.

dropped or cracked, and they can be thoroughly washed out – with disinfectant if necessary. Their main drawbacks are weight and fragility.

One enormous advantage of the purpose-built all-glass cage is its versatility. The vivarium may be made to almost any shape or size and can incorporate dividers, shelves and compartments for pumps, filters and so on if so desired. It can even be modified at a later date should the need arise. The way in which these all-glass aquaria are constructed has been described many times in the fish-keeping as well as the reptile-keeping literature, so there is no need to go into detail here. The best approach, where possible, is to tailor the dimensions and shape of the cage to the animals which are to live in it. Tree frogs, for instance, generally require tall vivaria which will accommodate branches and perhaps a living pot plant or two. Other species, such as the poison-dart frogs, Dendrobatidae, and several small salamanders, may benefit from running water, and an arrangement for providing this can often be incorporated into the initial design. Vivaria that are intended to be on show in the home often have a sloping front, enabling the inside of the cage to be viewed without distracting reflections appearing in the glass. Such a feature is also easily incorporated into the design and

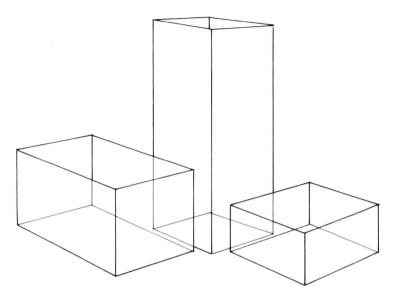

Fig. 1.   Glass cages of various shapes and sizes can easily be constructed using silicone aquarium sealant. Each cage can be tailor-made to suit the habits of the amphibians it is to accommodate and items such as partitions for land and water areas can be built in.

a similar arrangement will be useful if there is any likelihood that the cage will be used for photographing the inhabitants.

Also to be borne in mind at the outset are factors pertaining to the way in which the environment is to be controlled. Where equipment for heating, lighting and filtration is required, for instance, this can often be artfully hidden from view; at the same time it will need to be accessible for easy servicing. Bear in mind also that water and electricity make a lethal combination and so, above all, the set-up must be safe.

Described below are a number of fairly basic cage designs. They are not intended to be followed precisely but should be used as starting points from which individual requirements can be developed.

DESIGN 1: A BASIC 'SHOE-BOX' AQUARIUM/ VIVARIUM

The dimensions will be roughly in the ratio of 2:1:1 (length: width:height). Construction is of glass (thickness according to size) and silicone sealer. It is important that all the glass is cut accurately and that the edges are square. The base is laid on a flat surface and a thin, even bead of silicone is run along the back edge. The back of the cage is carefully placed on the edge of the base and supported by a heavy object placed behind it. A bead of sealer is now run along the edges of the base and up the edges of the back so that the sides can be put into position, one at a time. Once the back has been lined up with the sides, the two corners so formed should be held with masking tape. Now the front is fitted by applying sealer to the front edge of the base and the edges of the two sides and will also be held in place with masking tape once it is in position. When the sealer has begun to harden, usually after one or two hours, the joints can be made watertight by carefully running a bead of sealer right along every corner, using the nozzle on the container to achieve a smooth finish. The cage will be ready to use twenty-four hours later, possibly sooner, but should be well rinsed first to ensure that there are no traces of solvent or other impurities on the surface of the glass.

A very common and easy modification to this basic design is the fixing of a strip of glass across the tank to form a divider. This provides for a terrestrial as well as an aquatic area, which can be filled with gravel, moss and so on and furnished with hiding places and possibly living plants.

DESIGN 2: A SLIGHTLY TALLER CAGE WITH A REMOVABLE SLOPING FRONT

All the same precautions relating to the glass cutting and so on apply as for Design 1. The sides should be cut from a single rectangle of glass – this way the angles of both pieces will be exactly the same. The base, back and sides are put together as in Design 1. Then the bottom lip is fitted to the front of the cage: it should be the same length as the base and will therefore fit on to the edges of the two sides. The upper rail, on the other hand, will fit *inside* the two sides and so should be shorter than the base by an amount which is equal to the combined thickness of both sides. When the main construction is dry, a pair of small glass or perspex lugs can be fitted to the bottom rail to hold the front in place. The front can now be placed on top of the bottom rail and laid back against the sides and the top rail. If necessary, a small bulldog clip can be used to hold it here securely.

DESIGN 3: A SIMILAR CAGE, BUT WITH PROVISION FOR A CIRCULATING PUMP AND RUNNING WATER

Basic construction is, of course, as in Design 2. On completion of the cage a false floor is fitted over part of the base. The height of the floor will depend on the make of pump to be used, but it should not be higher than the bottom lip of the cage. A narrow piece of glass is stuck across one of the back corners of the cage. This will form the duct up which the pump's outlet pipe will go and should stop short of the top of the cage. The pump can be installed alongside the false floor, after which an arrangement must be made for preventing the animals from being drawn into the pump: this can be a strategically placed rock or a piece of perforated plastic but, whatever is used, it must not impede the flow of water towards the pump and the water level must, at all times, be above the pump. It is usual to cover the back of the cage with cork, peat blocks or rockwork in order to hide the pipes and cables and to enable the water to flow and drip down the back.

A rather more sophisticated system includes a power filter. This must be positioned outside the cage and so there needs to be an overflow outlet. The water runs through this to the power filter and is then forced back into the cage via one or more outlets towards the top of the cage. Needless to say, the overflow must be screened to stop any of the animals, eggs, larvae and so on from finding their way into the power filter. Furthermore, if this type of system is installed, care should be taken to see that, if the pump were to fail, the water would not all drain out of the tank.

Either system is suitable for temperate or tropical amphibians. For tropical species an aquarium heater/thermostat should be installed, preferably hidden but accessible.

Fig. 2. *Opposite above:* A simplified diagram showing one method of arranging running water. The pipework from the pump is hidden behind cork tiles, shown here partially removed. The false floor of the cage slopes so that the water runs off to a reservoir area from which it is recirculated. The pump would normally be hidden by careful arrangement of a piece of rock, driftwood or other material. Note that the water level must be sufficient to cover the pump completely.

Fig. 3. *Opposite below:* This system of running water incorporates a power filter. The water drains out of the cage before being filtered and recirculated.

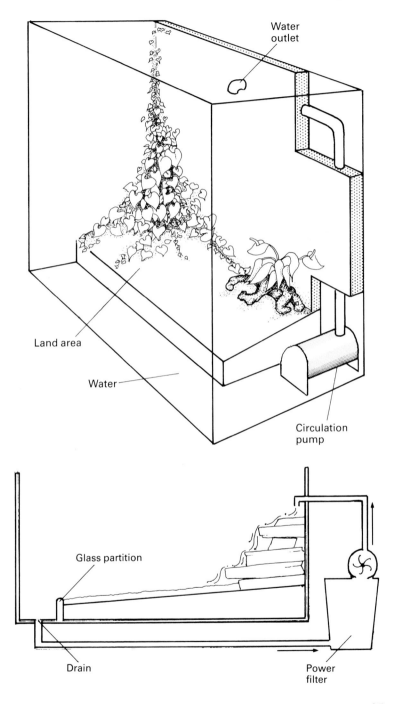

Water outlet

Land area

Water

Circulation pump

Glass partition

Drain

Power filter

Polystyrene platform

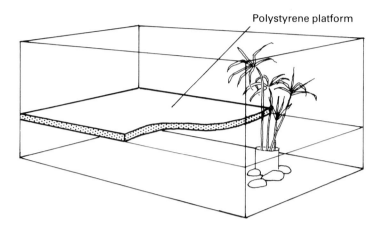

Fig. 4. A simple method of making a semi-aquatic cage or a breeding cage for arboreal or terrestrial amphibians. The platform consists of a piece of polystyrene cut to size and wedged or glued into one half of the cage at water level. Plants can be stood or grown in the water and food can be placed on the platform.

CAGE-FURNISHINGS

Most of the materials used to decorate the cages will be natural – branches, logs, plants and so on – and are discussed in Chapter 4. There are one or two artificial materials which have been used with varying degrees of success, however, and these are dealt with here.

Artificial materials are generally used for reasons of hygiene: substrates such as soil and leaf-litter can be difficult to keep clean, especially where animals are housed in high densities, perhaps as a result of successful breedings. Alternatives include paper towelling, such as kitchen roll, capillary matting as used by horticulturalists and foam rubber sheets or blocks. All these materials can be removed from the cages or containers easily and either discarded and replaced or rinsed out and re-used.

This system works well provided certain precautions are taken. Most importantly, *the materials must be free of chemical contaminants.* Bleaches are often used to 'improve' the appearance of paper towelling; capillary matting may be dyed green or black, or it may be printed with the makers' name, instructions for use and so on. More seriously, foam rubber intended for use in furniture upholstery is usually impregnated with various types of fire retardant, which leach out of the foam when it is moistened – all these substances are deadly toxic to amphibians. Unless you can be absolutely sure that the material in question does not contain any of the contaminants mentioned, artificial substrates should be avoided. 'Clean' alternatives include pea gravel which is available in a variety of sizes and which is cheap enough to be discarded if washing it becomes tedious. Horticultural peat, or peat substitutes such as coir (coconut fibre), are readily available in some parts of the world and these may be used provided they have not been 'fortified' with fertilizers. Similarly, moss collected locally, or Java moss, which can be grown in shallow containers, are safe alternatives.

CHAPTER 3

Controlling the Environment

The cage itself merely confines the amphibians. The environment inside the cage must be carefully controlled if the inhabitants are to thrive. Because of the nature of amphibians, however, there are two distinct types of environment which need to be considered: the aquatic and the terrestrial. Some principles, such as heating, are common to both whereas others, like filtration, apply to only one.

HEATING

If the cages are kept in a room in which the temperature is controlled to the correct level at all times, individual heating of cages will not be necessary. Similarly, if only local species are to be kept, or if the species come from areas with a similar climate to the prevailing one, no heating equipment will be required. Such a state of affairs occurs only occasionally, however, and it is usually necessary to provide individual heating to each cage.

Aquatic species are easily catered for: there are very many excellent aquarium heaters on the market, usually combined with a thermostat which can be pre-set at the desired level. Although models vary, the heater should be immersed in the water and should normally be fixed in a horizontal position. The rating of the heater should be appropriate to the capacity of the cage: powerful heaters in small volumes of water can quickly lead to disaster should the thermostat stick. For very large aquaria it may be necessary to install two heaters and thermostats in order to maintain the required temperature.

The actual temperature to which the water is heated will obviously depend on the species concerned. Tropical species and their larvae will require a temperature of around 27°C, subtropical ones around 20-25°C and temperate ones 5-20°C according to their origin (which is to say, supplementary heating is usually unnecessary). It may be necessary to alter the temperature throughout the year in order to duplicate natural climatic sequences, but tropical and sub-tropical species can normally be kept at a fairly constant temperature.

Terrestrial cages are almost as easy to heat as aquatic ones nowadays, thanks to the development of several items of purpose-built equipment. Thin heat-pads can be placed beneath the cage and their output controlled by a thermostat. The heat-pads give out a gentle heat over a wide surface and are therefore safe to use with glass cages. Furthermore, they will not normally overheat a cage even if the thermostat fails. The limitation of heat-pads is that, because of their low output, they will not be effective in heating cages with a thick layer of soil or other substrate. In such cases it may be possible to overcome the problem by attaching the heat-pad to the back of the cage (assuming that this is not covered with cork or some other insulating material). Other ways of heating terrestrial cages involve using a light-bulb or spotlight. These methods are rarely satisfactory because they tend to dry out the cage, and if plants are included in the set-up they will usually become scorched; it will also be difficult to control the temperature accurately. If fluorescent lights are included in the cage it will often be found that agile species, such as tree frogs, sit on the tubes, and this will give them some additional heating. In addition the starter units for these lights give out a fair amount of heat which can be utilized if they are placed up against the side of the cage, and it may be possible to capitalize on this heat source further by making a compartment inside the cage for the starter unit.

Semi-aquatic cages will be heated according to the proportions of water to land. Where most of the area is taken up with water, an aquarium heater and thermostat will probably serve. On the other hand, if water forms only a small part of the cage, a heat-pad will be required. Large cages, for instance those with running water, often benefit from aquarium heating *and* a heat-pad.

Aquatic heaters normally come complete with a thermostat, but heat-pads will require a separate thermostat to regulate their output. Vivarium thermostats can be of two basic types. First there is the simple on-off type, usually the least expensive, which can be used with all kinds of heating equipment, including light-bulbs, spotlights and so on (although the long-term effects of flashing light-bulbs, on the amphibians as well as on the viewer, are difficult to imagine). The other type of thermostat has proportional control: that is, as the temperature approaches the pre-set level, the power to the heater is reduced proportionately. Theoretically this gives a more accurate control as the temperature is maintained by trickling power to the heater in order to 'top up' the temperature. In practice both types of thermostat are effective, provided that they are well made and reliable and are used sensibly.

A further refinement is that of a thermostat which can be set at two temperatures: one for the day and another for the night. At present it is uncertain whether or not this degree of control is useful. There are so many factors involved in keeping and breeding amphibians that the advantages of day-night thermostats cannot easily be assessed, but there is plenty of scope here for experimentation and the small amount of extra cost involved would seem to make this equipment a worthwhile investment, especially where difficult species are involved.

Not all thermostats have the same capacity, however, and they must be matched to the heater: *using a heater which is too powerful for the thermostat can burn it out and may be hazardous*. Needless to say, all heaters and thermostats should be installed according to the maker's instructions.

Having installed the equipment to control the temperature, it will then be necessary to decide what temperature to aim at. This is not so easy. Unless detailed information already exists for the species in which you are interested, there will have to be some educated guesswork involved. As a general rule, species from temperate regions (northern Europe, northern North America) will require little or no heating provided their temperature does not drop to freezing point. At very low temperatures these species become inactive and would normally hibernate: if you decide to keep them active and feeding, it may be necessary to raise the temperature above 12°C or thereabouts by artificial means.

Intermediate – that is, subtropical – species should be maintained at a minimum temperature of around 15-20°C and tropical ones at about 20-25°C. Note that these are *minimum* temperatures: in order to keep these animals in the long term, or to breed them, it may be necessary to keep them rather warmer. Note also that these are guidelines, and attention should be paid to factors such as the altitude at which the species concerned lives. (To illustrate this point, the marsupial frog *Gastrotheca riobambae* occurs right on the equator in Ecuador: it lives at high altitudes, however, and is active at temperatures barely above freezing point.)

LIGHTING

The importance of lighting is often overlooked. Although it is true that amphibians, in general, prefer fairly subdued lighting, they are naturally subjected to seasonal variations in light intensity and daylength, and these factors must be considered if they are to be kept well. In addition, if living plants are included in the vivarium, these will also need adequate levels of light if they are to remain healthy.

The most suitable form of artificial lighting is almost always fluorescent. This gives out a good, even light without producing too much heat. Fluorescent tubes come in a range of sizes and power ratings. They are also available with different colour balances: some produce a 'cool' bluish light, while others are more heavily biased towards the 'warm', pinkish end of the spectrum.

There is evidence to suggest that at least some species of amphibians have a requirement for ultra-violet light, especially during development and around the time of their metamorphosis. If this is so, natural-spectrum tubes (producing a wide spectrum of light, including a small quantity of ultra-violet) should be advantageous; these are available under names such as 'Trulite' or 'Vita-lite'. Other models emit almost entirely ultra-violet rays and these are known as 'blacklights'. It is recommended that any serious attempt to raise amphibian larvae should include the provision of an ultra-violet light source, of either the natural-spectrum or the more powerful blacklight type. Although some species seem to be capable of developing normally without this, others show a high incidence of deformities and

7.   Fluorescent lights are the best choice for vivaria. Various colour temperatures are available, including 'Grolux', warm white and 'blacklights'. The last type gives out large amounts of ultra-violet radiation and is recommended for breeding amphibians.

deaths if it is not given. Furthermore, because the power of these lights is greatly reduced with distance, they should be mounted within about 20 cm of the surface of the water, and care should be taken to use waterproof fittings as supplied with aquarium lighting units.

If plants are to be grown in the cages housing the adult or larval amphibians, however, they will have the opposite requirement – for light from the 'warm' end of the spectrum. It may be necessary, therefore, to install two or more lights, including at least one for the benefit of the amphibians and another for the benefit of the plants. There is also room for experimentation here: several of the new energy-saving light systems designed for the home could probably be adapted for use in the vivarium – provided, of course, that safety considerations were not compromised.

The reproductive cycle of many amphibians is controlled by day length. They usually (though not always) breed in the spring when the days are growing longer. Day length should therefore be manipulated if breeding is to be attempted. This is a simple matter if a time-switch is fitted. It should be adjusted month by month so that the artificial days become longer in the spring and shorter in the autumn. It may even be possible to find a time-switch which senses light levels outside and turns the lights on and off accordingly – assuming that this regime is suitable for the species to be kept. Reproduction in tropical species, however, may not be linked to day length but to other factors such as temperature and humidity, and then the light cycle can be kept constant: that is, twelve hours on, twelve hours off, throughout the year.

HUMIDITY

Humidity can be controlled only very approximately, by adjusting the amount of ventilation and varying the amount of water which is put into the cage. If the cage is sprayed, the humidity will rise, but only for a while. Therefore, if a high humidity is required at all times, other measures must be taken. Reducing the amount of ventilation will increase the humidity (all other things being equal) but may also create a stagnant atmosphere which will not suit the amphibians (or any plants that happen to be in the cage). The most effective means of raising the humidity permanently is to install a system of running water. This will create a localized area of high humidity, allowing the species that requires this to find a spot which suits them. Methods of arranging it are described fully in Chapters 2 and 5.

THE AQUATIC ENVIRONMENT

Because almost all amphibians begin their lives as aquatic creatures (and some remain aquatic throughout their lives), the aquatic environment plays a special part in their care and breeding. Certain factors, such as temperature and light, are common to the aquatic and the terrestrial environment. Others, though, are peculiar to aquatic systems and must be considered separately.

What is meant by water quality?

Water quality is a generalized term covering a number of different aspects of water chemistry:

- the acidity or alkalinity of the water (pH)
- the amount of dissolved calcium and magnesium in the water (hardness)
- the amount of dissolved oxygen in the water
- the amount of organic material in the water
- the amount of dissolved inorganic salts and other impurities in the water.

Incorrect levels of any of the above can cause problems, especially to delicate amphibians such as larval forms. Although these factors are, to a large extent, interactive, it is convenient to deal with them one by one.

For aquatic amphibians, and the aquatic larvae (tadpoles) of terrestrial species, water is the medium with which the animals are continuously reacting. It is almost as though they are part of the water, rather than merely inhabitants. Thus, harmful as well as beneficial compounds in the water pass in and out of their bodies through the process of osmosis or through their gills, affecting their health and vitality. Furthermore, the nature of the water rarely stays the same for long: its chemistry is continuously changing as a response to the activities of the animals – that is, feeding, respiration, excretion – and any plants which may be present. Light also affects water chemistry under certain conditions, as does contact with certain inorganic substances. Although it is probably true that amphibians are tolerant of a wide range of water conditions, it is equally true that only by careful management of the aquatic environment will the optimum conditions be arrived at and, thereby, the healthiest animals produced.

The pH of the water

pH is a measure of the relative proportions of hydrogen ions (H^+) and hydroxl ions (OH^-) in solution in the water at any given time. In other words, it is a measure of acidity or alkalinity. Theoretically, pure water has a pH of 7, which is neutral. A pH lower than 7 indicates acid water and one higher than 7 indicates alkaline water. Very little research has been done on the pH requirements of aquatic amphibians, compared to that which has been carried out on fish, for instance. Most amphibians and their larvae probably prefer water which is either neutral or slightly acidic: that is, with a pH of between 6 and 7. Logically, for example, you would expect species that normally inhabit peat bogs, tropical swamps and so on to be adapted to acidic water since these environments are all affected by tannins leaching from decaying vegetation.

Determination of the pH of a sample of water is a very simple matter. Test kits, designed for aquarists, usually consist of a solution of indicator which must be added to the sample. The resulting colour of the sample is then compared to a set of standards from which the pH can be assessed. An even quicker method is to use indicator paper: a small piece of the paper is dipped in the water and the resulting colour again compared with those on a scale and the pH read off. This method is not as accurate as using a test solution, but it is quick and will give a result which is quite adequate for a routine check.

Regrettably, mains water supplies are rarely as reliable as the water authorities would like us to believe and the pH of water arriving through a household tap can vary greatly from day to day, or even from hour to hour. For this reason every batch of water should be tested before large amounts of it are used to set up a tank or to replace dirty water.

Water which is too alkaline can be rendered more acidic by the addition of tannins. Concentrates of these substances can be bought from aquarists' suppliers and are available under such names as 'Blackwater Tonic' and so on. Note, however, that their effect is not immediate and the treated water should be allowed to stand for a day or two before an accurate reading can be taken. Water which is too acidic can theoretically be corrected by the addition of sodium hydroxide (caustic soda). This is a dangerous substance which should be handled with great care and its use cannot be recommended except in the hands of experts. In practice it will rarely be found that the water supply is too acidic and, if alkaline water is required, perhaps to experiment with, it may be preferable to 'import' it from a natural source (for example from a spring in a chalk or limestone district) or to

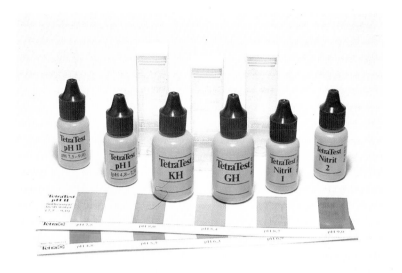

8. Various types of test kit are available for monitoring the pH and hardness of water.

manufacture it by trickling the water through limestone chippings or crushed coral over a long period.

A power filter, charged with the appropriate substances for correcting and buffering the water, can be beneficial in maintaining the correct pH. This is dealt with on pages 38–41.

Water hardness

The hardness of water is a measure of the amount of calcium and magnesium salts dissolved in it. Hardness can be divided into two types: temporary (sometimes known as carbonate hardness) and permanent. Temporary hardness is due to the presence of calcium and magnesium bicarbonates. These salts are formed when calcium and magnesium carbonates react with carbonic acid, a weak acid which is present in almost all supplies of water as a result of dissolved carbon dioxide. Although the bicarbonate salts dissolve easily, the carbonates do not, so when the carbonic acid is driven off (for instance, by boiling) the carbonate salts left behind drop out of solution – these are the substances which lead to a chalky deposit inside kettles, pipes and so on. The chemical equation for this reversible reaction is:

$$CaCo_3 + H_2CO_3 \leftrightarrow Ca(HCO_3)_2$$

$$MgCo_3 + H_2CO_3 \leftrightarrow Mg(HCO_3)_2$$

Permanent hardness is caused by other more soluble salts, especially calcium sulphate. These cannot be removed by boiling. The 'total hardness' occasionally referred to is the sum of the temporary hardness and the permanent hardness. Hardness is expressed as parts per million of calcium oxide (CaO), according to the German system, or parts per million of calcium carbonate ($CaCO_3$). The latter system is rarely used these days and water hardness is usually expressed in German degrees of hardness (°DH) where 0-5°DH is very soft and over 30°DH is very hard. Hardness test kits can be obtained for measuring temporary and permanent hardness.

The interplay between pH and hardness

As can be seen, calcium salts play a part in both the acidity and the hardness of water. It is no surprise, then, to learn that the two factors are usually linked: soft water is almost always acidic, whereas hard water is almost always alkaline. Although it is hard to establish how sensitive amphibians are to water hardness, if the pH of the water is maintained at a neutral or slightly acid level, the hardness factor will almost always look after itself. Indeed, several other factors affecting water quality are far more important in practice and, although it may be of academic interest to establish how hard the water is, attempting to maintain a particular level of hardness is usually pointless.

Dissolved oxygen

Oxygen is present in water in varying amounts. It gets there either by simple diffusion at the water's surface or from the respiration of aquatic plants, algae and bacteria. Oxygen will dissolve at the water's surface more readily if this is agitated: for instance, by an aerator. Although some oxygen will be absorbed from the bubbles themselves, the main function of aeration is to break the surface film, so facilitating gaseous exchange. At the same time the currents set up by aeration will help to distribute the oxygenated water from the surface to other parts of the water. A simple circulating system serves the same purpose, and the inclusion of a small cascade will also improve the oxygen uptake. In nature, cool, fast-flowing streams are likely to have a higher oxygen content than warm, still or sluggish bodies of water.

Oxygen resulting from biological activity will not be produced constantly: plants produce oxygen only as a result of photosynthesis and this can take place only in the presence of light. The oxygen content of a body of water will therefore fluctuate over a twenty-four-hour period, but will normally be greatest at the end of the day. Furthermore, the carrying capacity of water varies with temperature: at 10°C the water can hold almost twice as much oxygen in solution as it can at 30°C.

Oxygen is obviously important for the respiration of larval amphibians including neotonic forms, all of which breathe through gills. The natural habitat of the species concerned will control its tolerance: species from cool, fast-running mountain streams with a healthy growth of plants will obviously be used to far more oxygen than will tropical lowland species from more or less stagnant pools and puddles. For practical purposes, however, all aquarium water should be as well aerated as possible, not only for the benefit of the amphibians but also in order to maintain the colonies of bacteria which help to break down organic waste products into harmless substances.

Organic waste materials

Metabolic waste products and other organic material in the water, such as uneaten food, dead plants and so on, contain many substances, but the ones which are likely to cause most problems are the nitrogen compounds. These are broken down by a process known as nitrification, the end results of which are, ideally, nitrogen and nitrous oxide. It is the intermediate substances in the process of nitrification which can cause trouble. The whole process is part of the nitrogen cycle.

In the nitrogen cycle, the toxic chemicals found in organic waste materials are broken down in stages until they are turned into harmless compounds which are either used by plants or given off harmlessly into the atmosphere. The activities of two types of bacteria are involved. First, heterotrophic bacteria break the organic waste down into ammonia and similar chemicals. Then these chemicals, which are in themselves extremely toxic, are further broken down by autotrophic bacteria into the less toxic nitrites and, finally, nitrates. These last two compounds may be taken up and used by living plants, if present.

In an aquarium (or the aquatic section of a vivarium) the successful completion of the nitrogen cycle depends on three factors. In the first place, the amount of waste material must be minimized – this is achieved by not overcrowding the tank and not overfeeding the animals. Second, there must be sufficient surface area for the autotrophic (nitrifying) bacteria to accumulate. They will live on the sides of the tank but can be further encouraged if the available surface area is increased by the addition of rocks, gravel and so on. If the water is being circulated, the bacteria can live on many of the surfaces over which it trickles and, if the system is filtered, they can also live on the filter medium. Special materials are obtainable to increase the surface area of the latter and so encourage these useful bacteria; these materials can be used inside power filters, in open filters and in the tank itself. Finally the oxygen content of the water can be increased, either artifically using aeration or a cascade, or naturally by encouraging a healthy growth of plants, and this will encourage the bacteria and so speed up the nitrogen cycle.

If the system is overloaded with waste material or if insufficient oxygen is available, the system will switch to an anaerobic cycle, the end result of which will be extremely toxic substances, notably sulphur dioxide. Any unpleasant smells, black patches in the gravel, or other signs that decomposition is beginning to take place within the tank are an indication that the system is out of control.

How can water quality be maintained?

Although the above factors have been dealt with singly, as though they were unrelated to one another, it should be obvious that they are interconnected. For instance, the nitrogen cycle is dependent on the water's oxygen content, and the oxygen content may be dependent on the temperature and the amount of plant growth, which in turn may be dependent on the pH and/or hardness (and the amount of light available), and so on. Although it will not be possible, or even desirable, to maintain a totally stable aquatic environment, the various parameters should not be allowed to fluctuate beyond certain critical limits. These limits will depend on the species, but the herpetoculturalist should be in control at all times.

There are, fundamentally, two ways in which the quality of the water can be maintained within acceptable limits. It is possible to keep the water clean by removing all organic waste material at least once every day (by siphoning, for instance) and, at the same time, changing a proportion of the water. The aim here is to create a clinical, almost sterile environment for the amphibians or their larvae. Mechanical filtration may be helpful: these filters trap suspended particles, so removing them from the water. The usual way in which this is done is by allowing the water to trickle through filter wool, a block of foam rubber or some other form of wadding in which the particles become trapped. The filter medium must be replaced or washed regularly in order to maintain its effectiveness.

Alternatively, toxic products can be eliminated by harnessing the nitrogen cycle. This is achieved by encouraging the growth of plants and algae and allowing a healthy colony of nitrifying bacteria to develop on as many surfaces as possible. The latter method is less labour-intensive but requires rather more care. It is especially important to avoid overcrowding: a batch of tadpoles that may be adequately housed together at first, for example, may require dividing up into two or more batches as they grow and consume more food. Overfeeding is easily avoided: all the food placed in the tank should be consumed within an hour or so. It may be necessary to change from one food to another in order to encourage the animals to eat readily. The small amount of uneaten food, together with excretory waste products, should then be fairly easily dealt with by nitrifying bacteria.

Again, a filter may be useful, but in this case it should be of the 'biological' type. The purpose of these filters is not primarily to remove particles of waste but to provide sites within the filter on which the nitrifying bacteria can grow and to provide the bacteria with a steady supply of food by circulating water through the filter substrate. There are many models and designs available, each suited to a different situation and budget.

The simplest filters are the 'undergravel' types which use the gravel substrate of the tank as a site for the bacteria to colonize. The water is drawn through the gravel, usually by means of a simple airlift mechanism. Suspended particles are trapped in the gravel and are then available for processing by the bacteria. After a while the gravel will become clogged with larger particles and should be raked over and the particles removed mechanically by siphoning. An alternative system, involving 'reverse-flow' filtration, is more effective if used carefully. The water is pumped to the bottom of the layer of gravel, where there is a filter plate. The plate is perforated so that the water can pass through it and percolate up through the gravel. With this system any detritus settling on the gravel will stay on the top, where it can be easily removed, rather than being pulled through the gravel and trapped, thus clogging the filter. With reverse-flow undergravel filtration there should be some means of preventing pieces of detritus from being carried down under the filter plate, where they may block the holes and restrict water flow.

The larger models of mechanical filter can also be used as biological filters and you can improve their effectiveness by half-filling them with a porous substance such as crushed lava or the fragments of porcelain designed specially for the purpose. It is important to avoid damaging

9. Undergravel filters encourage the biological filtration of aquaria. They can cope with only low levels of pollutants, however.

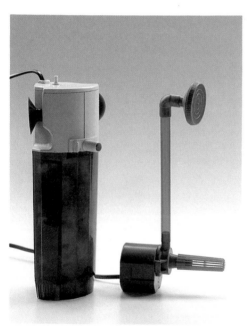

10. A small, submersible power filter (left) and a miniature circulation pump. Both these items are sold by aquarists' suppliers and can be used to good effect in aquatic and semi-aquatic vivaria.

the bacteria colony when cleaning out such filters, which should simply be rinsed through with water and then replaced – do not try to sterilize the filter! If a larger filter bed is required, this is simply built from a plastic container of the appropriate size filled with the required filter medium. It can be positioned above or below the level of the vivarium. Water is then pumped, siphoned or allowed to drain from the tank, trickled through the filter bed and returned to the vivarium.

Very large set-ups, those with running water or those consisting of several tanks often benefit from a power filter. This is installed outside the tank and water is forced through it and returned by a system of pipework. The actual designs vary with the make and model, but all have chambers which can be packed with a variety of filter substrates, some to act as mechanical pre-filters and others as biological filter beds. An additional advantage of these larger filters is the possibility of including natural substances such as peat or limestone chippings which can be used to adjust or buffer the pH and hardness of the water.

Chemical contamination

Any number of chemicals may find their way into the water in an aquarium, killing the occupants, and great care must be taken to avoid such contamination. Among the most common problems are those associated with clorine, which is added to the mains water supply by practically every authority in Europe and North America as a means of controlling bacteria levels. Although most adult amphibians are able to tolerate fairly high levels of chlorine, larvae are extremely sensitive. The simplest way of removing chlorine from the water is to allow it to stand for at least twenty-four hours or more. If it can be gently aerated, this will speed up the ageing process. Problems with chlorine (and other contaminants) can usually be minimized if complete water changes are avoided: it is far better to change, say, 10 per cent of the water every day, than 100 per cent every ten days.

Other contaminants which have an adverse effect on amphibians include those contained in disinfectants. As a general rule, amphibian cages should not be disinfected because it can be difficult to ensure that all traces are removed, even if the cage is thoroughly rinsed afterwards. If disinfectants must be used – to control a serious outbreak of disease, for instance – avoid surface-active agents, which are specifically designed to remain on surfaces even after rinsing.

Miscellaneous chemicals which should be avoided include aerosol sprays, especially those designed to kill insects, which should not be used anywhere near a cage containing amphibians (or other animals for that matter). Any glues, paints or varnishes used to construct the cage or to attach equipment or furnishings should be allowed to cure thoroughly before the cage is occupied. Where the use of paint and so on is unavoidable, such as during general redecorations, it may be advantageous to switch off any air pumps or circulation pumps until the fumes have dissipated; however, the animals should still be carefully watched for signs of distress.

CHAPTER 4

Natural Vivaria

In contrast to the care and maintenance of most reptiles, keeping amphibians often presents the opportunity (or necessity) of simulating their natural environment. The degree to which this can be achieved will be dependent on the species. For instance, small frogs, such as those belonging to the Dendrobatidae (poison-dart frogs) or the mantellas, are among the least destructive amphibians and can be housed along with a good selection of appropriate plants, including choice orchids, ferns and mosses. This type of set-up would, however, be totally inappropriate for robust species such as horned frogs, *Ceratophrys*, or burrowing species such as the spadefoot toad, *Scaphiopus*.

Terrestrial vivaria will be dealt with first, with notes on catering for aquatic species at the end of the chapter.

SUBSTRATES

Setting up a natural vivarium usually begins with choice of substrate. This covers the base and may act as a medium in which the amphibians can burrow. It may also function as the compost in which plants will be grown, although these are normally contained in pots or are grown as epiphytes (see below). The choice of substrates is large and will depend, to a large extent, on individual preference.

Sand and gravel substrates have the advantage of being easily obtained. They do little to enhance the appearance of the set-up, however, and are rarely used where aesthetics are the main consideration. An exception to this is in the maintenance of burrowing desert or semi-desert species such as the spadefoot toads and many of the true toads, genus *Bufo*. These species are compulsive burrowers and require an appropriate substate in which to indulge their behaviour. Horticultural silver sand is generally better than builder's sand, which tends to form a crust after it has been dampened. Sharp grit would

43

11. A selection of substrates including leaf-litter, orchid compost, quartz chippings and fine gravel can be used in vivaria.

appear to be a rather uncomfortable substrate in which to burrow, but grit comprised of small, rounded pebbles, such as the smallest grades of pea gravel, will usually be acceptable. For those in a position to obtain it, sand or gravel collected from a natural place will invariably look more natural – in the absence of a local desert to plunder, the fine gravel which collects on the bottom of streams is very suitable, but it should be well washed before use. If a few larger pieces of stone can be collected from the same locality, these will provide appropriate material for additional 'landscaping'.

Woodland species and those from rainforests and similar habitats require a more organic type of substrate. Leaf-litter is a common choice and will provide an excellent substrate provided it is not allowed to dry out, when it becomes dusty. A layer of larger pieces of dead leaves laid over the more broken-down material will look natural and will help to retain moisture. Pieces of bark will serve the same purpose and offer the advantage of providing hiding places. Artificial 'leaf-litter' such as peat, or one of the horticultural composts derived from such materials as coconut fibre and so on, can also be used if nothing better is available. Peat may be available in blocks, which can be arranged over the floor of the cage and also used to create a raised area, but the use of peat in non-essential areas such as this should be carefully considered in view of the concern over the destruction of natural habitats caused by its extraction. Slabs of tree fern root, used primarily in orchid cultivation and available through orchid suppliers, are equally convenient and are especially useful for the establishment of mosses and other epiphytes. This material, however, is very expensive and, again, the ecological consequences of its exploitation should be carefully considered. If any of these organic substances are used in conjunction with running water, tannic acid will be leached from them gradually, causing the water to become discoloured and acidic. This is not normally a problem as most species prefer slightly acid water, but care should be taken to ensure that a proportion of the water is changed occasionally in order to prevent too great a build-up.

It is possible to use more than one type of substrate, such as a layer of coarse gravel covered with a layer of leaf-litter, the gravel providing a drainage bed which prevents the leaf-litter from becoming waterlogged. This may be fine in theory, but in practice it will usually be found that the activities of the animals will quickly render the mixture into an untidy mass which serves no useful purpose at all. If drainage is thought to be necessary, it is far better to arrange this by building a false floor into the cage and allowing surplus water to trickle beneath it through a series of small holes. This particular feature can work very well in conjunction with a running water system.

12.   Tree fern root (left) and peat slabs can be used to landscape natural vivaria.

FURNISHINGS

One of the more enjoyable aspects of setting up a natural vivarium is the opportunity to hunt for attractive pieces of wood, rocks and so on with which it can be decorated. Driftwood and bogwood are often available commercially from aquarists' suppliers and, although rather expensive, are very suitable for use in the vivarium. Alternatively, suitable pieces of wood can be collected. Rocks are less appropriate for amphibian cages unless they are to be used in conjunction with a waterfall or other landscaped feature. Suitable pieces can be chosen from a variety of types, including slate, limestone and sandstone, but in the interests of appearance it is always better to stick to one type. If possible, buy or collect all the pieces from one location to ensure a good match. If rocks are to be used in conjunction with sand or gravel, they should also be of the appropriate type if at all possible.

Other furnishings are more of a practical nature. Unless a built-in water area is present, a bowl will be necessary. Glass is the best material for this because it can be thoroughly washed and sterilized if necessary. If active types of live food are to be used (and they almost certainly will be), it may be necessary to place a small twig or stone in the water to allow them to escape should they fall in. This should also be considered if there is any danger of the amphibians becoming trapped in the water bowl and drowning. Under certain circumstances it may be possible to place the amphibians' food in an additional bowl, but most types of live food will quickly escape and, in any case, giving the animals an opportunity to hunt throughout the cage for their food is more natural (and often more entertaining).

PLANTS

Planting a vivarium has a two-fold benefit. The plants, if well chosen and cared for, will undoubtedly enhance the appearance of the vivarium and complement the amphibian inhabitants. In addition they will provide hiding places and opportunities for climbing. Since many plants come from the same environments as the amphibians, they may also serve as indicators: if the conditions become unsuitable the plants will begin to suffer and this may be more immediately noticeable than any distress on the part of the amphibians. Plants require a suitable temperature and humidity in the same way that animals do. They also require adequate levels of light, and this must be of the right type as well as the correct intensity. Briefly, plants require light in the red and blue parts of the spectrum. Artificial lighting for plants often appears faintly pinkish to the human eye and suitable equipment is frequently named in such a way as to suggest its purpose, 'Grolux' being the most obvious example. In order to provide sufficient light, several tubes may be needed for large vivaria, and it may be advisable to raise the plants so that they are nearer to the top where the light intensity will be greatest. In practice this means growing the plants as epiphytes – that is, attached to pieces of wood – or providing a raised planting area, usually along the back of the set-up.

In addition the choice of species can have a substantial bearing on the long-term success or failure of the planting. Plants which need a great deal of light hardly ever do well in an artificial environment. Since these are mainly out-and-out desert species, however, they would rarely be considered in any case. The best choices are found among the ferns, orchids and bromeliads.

Types of plant

Bearing in mind the wide range of amphibians which may be available, the choice of plants is equally wide, if not more so. The choice will be restricted, however, by the prevailing conditions inside the cage, which will in turn be controlled by the species of amphibians to be kept. Aquatic vivaria are dealt with below and so the remaining options will consist of various combinations of temperature (cool or warm) and humidity (dry, moist and wet). These are dealt with in turn, although it must be understood that there are no firm dividing lines and that one class of conditions will often merge into the next. Indeed, many set-ups will contain areas of two or more different types.

COOL, DRY CONDITIONS
For practical purposes there are no amphibians which require these conditions and so planting is not considered.

COOL, MOIST CONDITIONS
These conditions are most suitable for a range of amphibian species from northern latitudes: for instance, several species of true toad, genus *Bufo*; the midwife toad, *Alytes obstetricans*; some tree frogs, genus *Hyla*; and some salamanders such as the European fire salamander, *Salamandra salamandra*, and a number of the North American species of *Ambystoma* and *Plethodon*.

Appropriate planting would consist of a wide range of small ferns such as those belonging to the genus *Asplenium* (spleenworts). Other suitable species include ivies, especially some of the cultivated varieties with smaller leaves and less vigorous growth, and club-mosses such as *Selaginella*. Several species and varieties of all these plants can be obtained easily through garden centres. In addition, pieces of bark, logs and so on which are collected for the vivarium will often already be colonized by native mosses; if these can be encouraged to grow, they should be used wherever possible.

COOL, WET CONDITIONS

A number of European and North American amphibians live in puddles or around the edges of small ponds and streams and these are most suited to cool, wet conditions. They include frogs such as cricket and chorus frogs, genera *Acris* and *Pseudacris*, and terrestrial stages in the life-cycle of many newts, especially those belonging to the European and Asian genus *Triturus*, the beautiful North American *Pseudotriton* species and the oriental species *Tylotriton*. These conditions are also ideal for newly metamorphosed amphibians, for the time when they are making the transition between an aquatic and a terrestrial way of life.

Plants for these species are best chosen from among the selection of marginals offered by aquarists' suppliers and garden centres. Suitable small species include sedges, genus *Carex*; *Lysimachia nummularia* (creeping Jenny); and the aroid *Acoris gramineus*. A number of other small marsh plants are often sold as tropical aquarium plants and some of these tolerate, or even prefer, cooler conditions than the vendors would have us believe. In many cases it is preferable to leave the plants in pots, standing them in few centimetres of water with a gravel substrate.

Insectivorous plants, many of which are now freely available, are ideally suited to wet conditions and will grow in nutrient-poor soil such as peat. The main problem here is that the plants may compete for food with the amphibians and some of the larger species are capable of trapping and 'eating' small frogs. Avoid, therefore, the pitcher plants, *Sarracenia* and *Nepenthes* species; the Venus flytrap, *Doinaea muscipula*; and the larger sundews, *Drosera*. Choose instead from the bladderworts, such as *Utricularia sandersonii*, and the butterworts, *Pinguicula*. The latter have sticky leaves but would not harm any but the very smallest, newly metamosphosed froglets.

WARM, DRY CONDITIONS

Although amphibians cannot tolerate completely dry conditions for any length of time, a fairly dry environment is appropriate for some of the more specialized species such as several toads, including spadefoot toads, from deserts and other warm regions. Because all these species tend to burrow, devising a suitable planting scheme can be difficult. There are, however, a number of plants which can be protected by planting in pots which are then buried in the substrate. Placing pebbles or flat pieces of rock around the crown of the plants will minimize the possible risk of their being uprooted. Tough plants, such as the houseleeks, *Sempervivum*, and the stonecrops, *Sedum*, are most suitable if enough light can be provided. Drought-adapted plants can be grown if the cage is well ventilated and all moisture is kept to one end, with the plants grouped towards the driest end. For those with a subsidiary interest in the plants themselves, several other succulent plants could be tried out but very often their insistence on high levels of light is a drawback. Plants which are suffering from insufficient light become drawn, bending abnormally towards the strongest source of light and growing pale in colour.

WARM, MOIST CONDITIONS
This category and the next are the areas where appropriate planting can completely transform the appearance of the vivarium. Many 'house plant' species thrive in warm, humid surroundings, but many of them become too rampant under such ideal conditions. Notable exceptions are the dwarf strain of *Spathifolium* (peace lily) which can usually be counted on to survive even when trampled by robust amphibians, and several small ferns, especially compact species such as hare's foot. A small species of flamingo flower, *Anthurium* species, is sometimes available and this makes an excellent choice as it can be grown in the ground or attached to wood. No doubt there are many other suitable species available and there is plenty of room for experimentation here. Of the larger plants, only suitable for vivaria of the most ambitious proportions, the broad, dark green leaves of any of the many species of *Philodendron* make spectacular plantings.

For the more adventurous a large number of small orchids are suitable. Species chosen should be from the 'intermediate' selection offered by specialist nurseries (orchids sold by garden centres are usually of the more showy hybrid varieties which are delicate and tend to look untidy when not in flower). Among the dozens of genera to look out for the following are recommended: *Odontoglossum* (smaller species only), *Oncidium*, *Masdevallia*, *Pleurothallus* and *Coelogyne*. The cheaper species are usually the best choice – they tend to be the ones which are most easily grown and propagated. Similar conditions are required by several of the small and medium-sized bromeliads (air plants) of which the Tillandsias are especially recommended. Large bromeliads such as

13.   A rainforest-type vivarium in which poison-dart frogs are kept together with a variety of mosses, ferns, orchids and bromeliads.

the Vriesias and Guzmanias are suitable only for large vivaria, but if there is room for them their central 'vases' will provide excellent hiding places for small frogs and some species will even breed in them.

All orchids mentioned above, as well as the bromeliads, can be grown as epiphytes and this is a most suitable method for planting a vivarium intended for small frogs, for example. In their natural habitat these plants cling to the branches of trees in order to capture as much light as possible in the highly competitive rainforest communities. They can be grown on branches, driftwood and so on, and should be tied in using a ball of sphagnum moss and some nylon fishing line. It will take a while before their roots begin to grip the wood and during this period the plants should be protected from boisterous amphibians: it may be desirable to set up a separate cage for establishing the plants and then moving them, complete with their branch, to an occupied cage once they are established and growing well. Although they will benefit from occasional spraying once installed, conditions inside the cage should ensure that they will thrive. Some may even flower regularly, although their main contribution to the appearance of the vivarium will be their neat, dark green foliage. An often overlooked

14. *Tillandsia* species are sometimes known as airplants. They are epiphytic and ideally suited for attaching to driftwood and similar material in vivaria.

15. A miniature orchid, *Oncidium cheirophorum*. A number of easily obtained species of small orchids will grow and flower in well-designed vivaria.

aspect of orchid (and bromeliad) cultivation is their requirement for fresh air – warm, stagnant conditions do not suit them and they will quickly rot or succumb to disease if air does not circulate around them. As it happens, the same requirement for good ventilation applies to most tropical amphibians and so this factor should not prevent orchids and frogs from thriving in the same cage.

WARM, WET CONDITIONS

Most tropical frogs prefer moist rather than wet conditions, but in a large vivarium, especially one with a waterfall or other system for circulating water, there will be areas which are rather wetter. Several of the plants mentioned above can be kept here, provided that their roots are kept free of standing water; for example, they may be grown as epiphytes. In addition a number of plants sold as aquarium species will also grow out of the water as long as they are not allowed to dry out completely. Included in this selection, and very useful in the vivarium, is Java moss, *Vesicularia dubyana*, which will grow on damp wood and even over rocks if these are kept permanently wet – by spray from a waterfall, for instance.

One useful trick to encourage the growth of tropical and subtropical mosses is to use pieces of tree fern root in the set-up. When warm water is trickled over these constantly, and the level of light and temperature is adequate, mosses will often begin to grow over them spontaneously. They arise from spores which settled on the root while it was still *in situ*, and which had laid dormant for many years, awaiting suitable conditions for germination. (The roots of tree ferns build up above ground and, as the plant grows, support the crown well above ground level, serving the same function as the trunks of trees and shrubs.)

THE SEMI-AQUATIC SET-UP

A number of species of frogs and toads require accommodation which gives them a choice of terrestrial and aquatic areas. The fire-bellied toads, *Bombina* species, are the most obvious example, although there are several others. The most convenient way of arranging this is to use a glass aquarium-type cage with a glass divider. The divider can be permanently fixed in place with silicone aquarium sealer or it can be made removable, in which case it is kept in place by a plastic channel or with heavy rocks or bricks placed on each side. Both systems have advantages and disadvantages. If the divider is permanent and water finds its way into the 'dry' area, as a result of the activities of the animals for example, the substrate will soon become waterlogged and will need to be replaced. If the divider is temporary, on the other hand, water will quickly seep through and so the land area will need to be filled with pea gravel or a similar free-draining material. An alternative method is to create a glass platform as described in the section on running water (page 55). Whichever method is used, the animals must have some means of climbing up out of the water – either a piece of flat rock forming a ramp or a piece of driftwood strategically placed.

Furnishing and planting semi-aquatic vivaria will follow the same general patterns for aquatic set-ups on the one hand and moist or wet set-ups on the other. A very useful plant for this type of cage is *Cyperus alternifolius nana*, a small form of umbrella plant which grows to about 40 cm in height. It should be left in its pot and stood in the aquatic section. If the top of the pot is level with the surface of the water, an additional land area will be produced. Java moss is also useful as it will grow both in and out of the water and may be used to hide the divider.

AQUATIC SET-UPS

There is a mass of popular literature concerned with the setting-up and planting of aquaria and some ideas can be gleaned from that source. Otherwise the landscaping of an aquarium is very much a question of personal taste. If the set-up is to look natural, a uniform substrate of pea gravel should be avoided: alternatives are granite or basalt chippings, which should be of varied size with a few larger chunks included. Well-washed river gravel looks very effective, as does a layer of larger pebbles or small cobbles. Alternatively, consider a layer of dead leaves as a substrate, especially for species such as the sirens, aquatic caecilians and the *Pipa* frogs which come from swamps. Driftwood or water-logged roots fished out of ponds and streams are ideal for providing hiding places, and some species of plants, notably Java moss and Java fern, *Microsorium pteropus*, will grow well if attached to wood, although both of these are suitable only for warm conditions.

Other plants include a wide range of the more robust species sold for cold-water or tropical aquaria, according to the type of amphibians which are to be housed. For breeding newts, plants such as Canadian pondweed, *Elodea canadensis*, are useful as the females will lay their eggs on the leaves. Floating plants are especially useful for most species as they will filter the light and provide security for the amphibians. Among the best are the ferns *Salvinia auriculata* and *Ceratopteris thalictroides* (tropical) and *Salvinia natans* (cool water). If the aquarium houses frog and toad tadpoles, however, most species of

16. Aquatic plants help to maintain good water quality and may also provide a necessary substrate for egg laying.

plants will soon be eaten and so only easily replaced and quick-growing species should be used.

Since the nitrogen cycle relies heavily on healthy, growing plants (see Chapter 3), every effort should be made to provide ideal conditions.

CREATING A WATERFALL

The addition of running water not only increases the visual interest of the vivarium but will also help to create suitable conditions for a number of amphibians as well as plants. The system may be closed or open, and in either it is important to ensure that pieces of debris do not find their way into the pump as they will quickly destroy the internal mechanism. This effectively means that soil, peat and so on are unsuitable for such units unless they are restricted to pots in which plants are grown.

A closed system is the most convenient and can be easily and cheaply installed. The availability of compact, reliable circulation pumps has greatly helped in this area: several models are sold through aquarium suppliers at reasonable cost. The design of such a set-up should be considered when the cage is being built: this is far easier

17. *Salvina auriculata* is a small floating fern which is invaluable for use in aquatic and semi-aquatic vivaria. It diffuses the light and conditions the water as well as providing cover for the inhabitants.

than trying to modify a cage which may be the wrong size or shape. The land area is created by building a glass platform, sloping slightly to allow the water to run into a reservoir area, which can be along the front of the cage or at one end. The level of the water in the reservoir must be sufficient to cover the circulation pump at all times. If there is any danger of the amphibians or their larvae being sucked into the pump it should be housed in a separate compartment, ensuring that water can flow to it quickly enough to keep the circulation going. There must also be access to the pump in case servicing is required.

In an open system the water is drawn from the set-up by means of a drain or overflow leading to a pump which is positioned outside the cage (usually on a lower level). The pump in this case may also serve to force the water through a filter bed (that is, a power filter) before it is pumped back to the top of the tank. This system is suitable only for large set-ups.

Whichever system is used, arranging the rockwork and so on is very much a matter of personal taste, coupled with a degree of artistic skill. An attempt should be made to disguise the pipework taking the water from the pump to the top of the cage. Small rocks can be held in place with silicone sealer to prevent their being dislodged. Alternatively, rocks can be dispensed with altogether if the back of the vivarium is covered with flat pieces of cork or tree fern root. Then the water is fed to the top and allowed to trickle down over the surface. This will encourage the growth of mosses and ferns. Small orchids and bromeliads can be attached to branches placed in the cage and the humid conditions and constantly moving air, created by the circulating water, should ensure that they will thrive.

A 'RAIN' MACHINE

Whichever type of circulation system is used, it is a fairly easy matter to convert the waterfall into a 'rain machine'. Instead of trickling from a spout, the water is forced through a sprinkler bar, as used in connection with some power filters. If the pump is then wired up via a time-switch it can be made to simulate rain once or twice each day, creating the right conditions to encourage certain species of frogs to breed.

It is important to note that evaporation will be very high in any of the above systems. It is essential, therefore, to regularly replace any water so lost otherwise the pump will run dry.

CHAPTER 5

Outdoor Vivaria

The idea of keeping amphibians outdoors has several attractions. There is usually a greater availability of space, allowing the animals to behave more naturally; they benefit from natural sunshine and a certain amount of natural food; a well-designed outdoor vivarium will enhance the garden; and, last but not least, they will require little in the way of conventional cleaning out!

The potential for keeping amphibians in this way will depend primarily on the climate. Montane salamanders will not thrive in southern Arizona any more than tropical frogs will thrive in northern England. In most parts of the world, however, it should be possible to keep an interesting selection, especially if the climate can be 'improved' to some extent by adding a glass lid during the colder months, shade during the warmest months, or whatever is appropriate.

The scope is very large. Even a small, open garden pond can provide a home for a number of species, whereas a more sophisticated enclosure can be designed to house a range of species, including some which would otherwise be difficult to maintain. Again the enclosure may be used to house amphibians all year round with a minimum of attention, or to intensively rear fairly large numbers of animals during the warmer months only.

PONDS

For most amphibians the pond will be the most important habitat. Equally important will be the area immediately surrounding the pond, through which they must travel to gain access to the water itself. Methods of constructing ponds are described in gardening books and books on fish keeping. For the purposes of amphibian keeping, however, there are a few additional points worth remembering.

The best material for making the pond is undoubtedly butyl. Sheets of this material can be purchased in a variety of widths and the required length is usually cut from a roll. For most purposes the pond should be situated in an open part of the garden so that the water warms up quickly. This will also avoid problems with falling leaves in the autumn. If the pond is to be used for the amphibians throughout the year, it will need to be about 45 cm deep in parts so that the water does not freeze right to the bottom. A shallower area should also be constructed, because some species prefer to spawn in shallow water. If possible, a damp area for marginal plants should be arranged around part of the pond; this will enable newly metamorphosed frogs, toads and salamanders to emerge from the water without risk of predation. If a rockery or log pile can be built close by, there will be plenty of places for the amphibians to forage, hide and hibernate, and this will prevent them from straying too far from the pond during their terrestrial phase, even where the pond does not form part of an enclosure.

The pond should be well stocked with aquatic plants, *Elodea crispa* being an ideal species both for oxygenating the water and for providing a suitable egg-laying medium for newts. This can be planted in a special pond basket sunk to the bottom of the pond or allowed to root in a few centimetres of soil scattered over the bottom. Plants with floating leaves, such as lilies, *Potamogeton* species and water soldier, will provide cover for the amphibians and will also filter the light reaching the water and thereby control the growth of algae. An effort should be made to ensure that duckweed is not introduced to the pond or it will quickly blanket the whole of the surface, starving submerged species of light completely. Management of the pond should consist merely of removing excess plants in the autumn when most of the amphibians will have left the water. Algae is not normally a problem in a well-balanced pond but there may be an algal bloom when the pond is first filled: it will correct itself once the higher plants start to grow and excess nutrients have been used up.

It is a good idea to introduce some invertebrates to the pond shortly after it has been set up (they may arrive along with the plants anyway). Species such as *Daphnia* will help to clear the water and will form a useful reservoir of food for newts. Larger invertebrates, such as pond snails and the larvae of flying insects, can also be introduced. Although damsel and dragonfly larvae will eat some tadpoles, they need not be excluded altogether because they add to the interest of the pond while taking only a small proportion of the tadpoles (and the weaker ones at that). Fish (and terrapins), on the other hand, have no place in a pond which is intended primarily for amphibians because they make large inroads on the larval population, sometimes wiping them out altogether.

Such a pond is fairly conventional in that the amphibians will be free

18.   A garden pond built for amphibians by Geoff Trinder, Lincolnshire.
A well-designed garden pond will encourage local species amd may form part
of a much larger wildlife garden, as here.

to come and go and there will be little control over numbers. It is best
suited to the 'keeping' of local native species. Note that, in the United
Kingdom, it is against the law to introduce exotic species of amphibians
into the wild, and so housing them in a garden pond which is not
enclosed may be an infringement of this law.

If a low wall is built around the pond and its immediate surroundings, the scope is increased several-fold. Exotic species can be kept, in
the knowledge that they are not going to disappear next door (where
the neighbours' pond may be more attractive to them) as soon as your
back is turned. It is also easier to control predation by birds, rats and,
especially, domestic cats. If the last problem gets out of hand, the only
remedy is to fix netting across the enclosure. The enclosure wall can
be made from sheets of clear plastic (perspex or acrylic) or glass, or a
more permanent structure can be made from timber, bricks or concrete
blocks. Some precautions should be taken to ensure that the inhabitants
cannot burrow out and that predators, especially rats, cannot burrow
in. Strips of sturdy plastic mesh can be buried to a depth of about 30
cm below ground level or, in the case of a permanent wall, concrete
footings can be laid.

19.   Many species fare better in outside enclosures than they do in indoor vivaria. The natterjack toad, *Bufo calamita*, is a case in point, although it should be noted that this is a protected species in the United Kingdom.

20.   The European fire salamander, *Salamandra salamandra*, in all its forms, is an ideal inhabitant for a cool, moist and shady outdoor enclosure. Once settled in, it will breed year after year with little attention.

Such an enclosure, with a fairly large pond, would be suitable for a number of types of frog, especially the many *Rana* species, toads, genus *Bufo* and most of the newts, such as those belonging to the New World genus *Triturus* and the North American genus *Notophthalmus* as well as certain of the ambystomid salamanders, depending on the climatic conditions. Some amphibians which are suitable for outdoor enclosures prefer smaller ponds and here the amount of water can be scaled down and the amount of rockery or undergrowth increased proportionately. These species include the European fire-bellied and yellow-bellied toads, *Bombina bombina* and *B. variegata*; the midwife toad, *Alytes obstetricans*; the parsley frog, *Pelodytes punctatus*; and the European fire salamander, *Salamandra salamandra*. All of these species are ideal subjects for outdoor enclosures, although there are plenty of others.

In an enclosed environment, the amphibians are obviously unable to stray very far in their search for food or for hibernation sites. This must be overcome, firstly by adding an appropriate amount of suitable food insects to the enclosure regularly, and secondly by ensuring that there is at least one area where the amphibians can burrow down below the frost level. The latter is best arranged by exacavating a pit (perhaps at the same time as the pond is dug) and filling it with rocks or brick rubble. The spaces created will be ideal sites, provided the water table does not flood them. Another solution is to bury one or more polystyrene boxes in the enclosure and arrange entry to them through earthenware drainage pipes. Again it is important to ensure that the chambers cannot flood and that the entrances to the tubes are above the water table and sheltered. If a single large flat slab is laid over the lid of each box, it will be possible to inspect the chamber during the winter hibernation in order to check on the health of the animals and, at other times, to replace any dead leaves and so on which are acting as bedding. Under extreme conditions it may be necessary to remove the animals to a more sheltered site for a few weeks.

PLANTING

A good selection of plants will make the enclosure more attractive and will also serve the useful purpose of giving the inhabitants places to hide. Flowering plants will attract a wide range of flying insects during the summer, adding to the general interest and providing a good variety of extra food for the amphibians. The types of plants will obviously depend on the conditions. For shady, damp enclosures, grasses, sedges and rushes may well form the dominant type of vegetation. Ferns are also attractive and many spectacular species, such as the royal fern, *Osmunda regalis*, will do well in the conditions described, although they may grow too high if the enclosure is covered.

If the enclosure is more rocky, with one or two pools scattered among the rocks, there is a wide selection of alpine plants from which to chose. Cushion- and mat-forming species, such as thrift, *Armeria*, various saxifrages and the alpine cranesbills, *Geranium* species, are very useful, as are more shrubby plants such as the heathers, *Erica*. A visit to a garden centre or a specialized alpine nursery will produce plenty of options, but it may be a good idea first to consult a basic reference work in order to investigate the requirements of some of the plants and their eventual size.

Maintenance of the enclosure, other than that of the pond, which has already been mentioned, will consist of keeping the plants under control, especially larger species which may grow above the level of the wall and so provide a possible route to freedom for the amphibians. Otherwise, the build-up of dead leaves and other debris can be beneficial, providing as it does more opportunities for hiding and hibernation sites and, again, encouraging insects which the amphibians will use as a supplementary food supply. If the pond freezes over in the winter, it can be a good idea to keep one area free of ice in case any of the

21.   Houseleeks, *Sempervivum* species, and similar rockery plants are good for dry areas in outdoor enclosures as they are practically indestructible and their flowers attract insects during the summer.

animals have hibernated on the bottom: although they will usually withstand the cold, they may suffocate to death if a layer of ice prevents oxygen exchange at the surface. An alternative, essential if delicate species are included in the set-up, is to cover part or all of the enclosure with glass during the colder months. In severe conditions, additional protection can be provided by placing a layer of straw or bracken over the areas where the amphibians are known to hibernate and sacking or old pieces of carpet over the glass cover.

If the amphibians breed successfully, they will probably produce more larvae than can be reared in the pond(s) provided, even allowing for some predation by insects, newts and their larvae and so on. A proportion should be removed, therefore, and reared separately in temporary ponds or aquaria, or disposed of to other herpetologists. On no account should the larvae of exotic species be disposed of indiscriminately in local ponds or streams: they may compete unfavourably with local species and become pests. In the United Kingdom and in parts of North America, such spurious introductions are, in any case, illegal.

One potential drawback to keeping frogs and toads outside should perhaps be mentioned. If they do well and breed, this happy event will often be preceded by several weeks of calling. There is much variation in both the tunefulness and the volume of their calls and, whereas the neighbours may be faintly amused, enchanted even, by the dainty, bell-like voice of midwife toads, the raucous trill of tree frogs or the pulsating staccatos of some of the *Bufo* species, reminiscent of a small outboard motor housed in a large biscuit tin and designed to carry for several hundred metres, may not be regarded with such enthusiasm!

CHAPTER 6

Food and Feeding

All adult amphibians are carnivorous (the one exception being a tropical frog which can be ignored for our purposes). Of the amphibian larvae, all newt and salamander larvae are predatory, as are the larvae of some frogs, including most of the Dendrobatidae (poison-dart frogs). Otherwise, frog and toad tadpoles are largely herbivorous, feeding on a wide variety of plant material (including algae) and on bacteria.

FEEDING ADULT AMPHIBIANS

The menu of wild amphibians is enormous. Basically they will eat anything which is small enough to fit into their large mouths and which they can catch. This includes insects and other invertebrates such as worms, other species of frogs and toads, small reptiles and small mammals. For amphibians in captivity it is important to provide as varied a diet as possible. A number of insect species are cultured and sold commercially for the purpose of feeding livestock, including amphibians.

Crickets are probably among the most commonly offered and they are a good food item provided appropriate sizes are used. If the crickets are too large, they will be ignored and may become a pest in the cage, destroying plants and bothering the amphibians. The same applies if an excess of crickets is placed in the cage, since many of them will escape the amphibians and may set up home in inaccessible crevices. Crickets, then, must be used in moderation, and should be fed only in numbers which can be consumed more or less straightaway. If they are placed in a refrigerator for ten minutes before being tipped into the cage, they will be less lively and the amphibians will have a greater chance of catching and devouring them before they disperse.

Mealworms are also easily obtained but their usefulness is rather limited. They do not form a balanced diet, being low in digestible

22. The basic menu: a cricket liberally dusted with a multi-vitamin and mineral powder.

calcium, and so amphibians fed exclusively on them soon develop deficiencies. Toads, in particular, are very fond of them, however, and they can be given sparingly.

Waxworms are the larvae of a moth which is a pest in bee-hives. They are relished by almost all species of amphibians and are an excellent food item. Their main drawbacks are that they are expensive (unless cultured at home) and they do not survive for long in the moist environment of an amphibian cage. They are also good climbers and will walk up the glass sides of the cage. If the vivarium contains agile species such as the tree frogs this is no problem, but the insects may crawl out of the reach of other species. Escaped waxworms can be destructive around the house. In the absence of their preferred food they will eat wood, books and even plastic! Care must be taken, then, to ensure that, once they are placed in a cage, they are all eaten. Tebo worms are rather similar to waxworms but are collected (in South America) rather than cultured, which tends to make them rather expensive.

Flies are an underused resource. All amphibians eat them readily and they seem to provide a good staple diet. Several species are available, cultured for the angling industry rather than as a live food. This makes them cheap and readily available. The larvae (maggots) should be purchased in small quantities and kept warm until they pupate. A number of pupae can be placed inside a ventilated plastic container, a fisherman's bait-box being the most obvious choice, and kept warm until they emerge. A small hole is cut in the top and the flies can be allowed to crawl out into the vivarium. The art is in putting the right number of pupae into the box in the first place – if there are too many the hatched flies will fill the vivarium, so that it is difficult to open it without their escaping. A better way, though more trouble-some, is to place batches of the pupae in plastic beakers. When the flies emerge the beakers are put into the refrigerator for about fifteen minutes to chill their occupants, which can then be tipped into the vivarium without risk of escape. While they are in the chilled state it is easy to sprinkle vitamin and mineral supplements over the flies (see below).

Fruit flies, *Drosophila*, can be used as food for very small species of amphibians and for the young of others. Although they can be cultured at home, it is a tedious and messy business and is probably best left to those with very large collections. Small quantities can be purchased along with enough medium (food) to keep them going for several weeks. If the culture is kept in a warm place a few flies will emerge every day and these can be shaken straight into the vivarium.

Earthworms are available from some live-food suppliers or they may be collected during the warmer months. Some amphibians, including

23. Not all amphibians restrict themselves to an insectivorous diet, a fact which should be borne in mind when handling larger specimens!

toads and most aquatic species, are very keen to eat them, but others find them too difficult to handle.

Other food items which can be collected include spiders, small flies, aphids, beetles and so on. Hand-collecting is tedious but there are several techniques for gathering large numbers of insects more efficiently. The most productive method is to use a sweep net, which can be swished backwards and forwards through clumps of undergrowth, nettles being a good hunting ground. As soon as there is a reasonable catch in the bottom of the net it can be transferred to a glass or plastic collecting jar. All that remains to be done is to ensure that there are no potentially harmful species, such as large wasps and predatory spiders, among them and tip them into the vivarium. Aphids, which are an excellent first food for small, newly metamorphosed frogs, can be transferred to the vivarium by snipping off shoots of the infested plants. Beware that insects which are collected may have come into contact with insecticide sprays, which are harmful to amphibians. If possible, collect them from your garden, which should be kept free of such chemicals. Alternatively, find an area of waste land which is heavily populated with insects – the chances are that this will have been ignored by sprayers. Do not, however, be tempted to forage around the local nature reserve, however rich a hunting ground it is!

FOOD SUPPLEMENTS

The purpose of food supplements is to compensate for the lack of variety in the diet of captive animals. Theoretically, if a wide variety of food, including 'wild' insects, is given, supplements should not be necessary, but this is rarely the case. By dusting the food regularly with any one of a number of proprietary reptile and amphibian vitamin and mineral supplements, dietary imbalances can normally be corrected. Unfortunately, because of our lack of detailed knowledge in the area of amphibian nutrition, it is difficult to say in what quantities or how often supplements should be provided. As a rule cultured food species tend to be very low in calcium but higher in phosphorus. Since a suitable calcium:phosphorus ratio is one of the fundamental requirements of all animals, it is fairly safe to assume that supplements which are high in calcium but low in phosphorus are the most useful. All good quality supplements on the market are labelled with a breakdown of their constituents.

Another requirement about which little appears to be known is that of vitamin D. In certain reptiles lack of this vitamin leads to poorly formed bones, infertile eggs and deformed young. Breeding results among some species of amphibians seem to indicate that their requirement may be similar. Vitamin D is manufactured by most animals when they are exposed to ultra-violet radiation: for example, that which is contained in natural sunlight. It is well known that in reptiles exposure to lights which emit ultra-violet rays (coupled to the administration of extra calcium) will cure deficiency problems. A few inconclusive experiments with amphibians would seem to point in the same direction, with the most vulnerable stage being from around the time the tadpoles metamorphose until they are about half-grown. It seems reasonable to assume that species whose natural habitats are shady, or which are nocturnal, would have a lesser requirement for vitamin D than those which expose themselves to direct or indirect sunshine, and this may well be the case. Nevertheless, if serious breeding is contemplated, it is a good idea to invest in the correct equipment. A number of fluorescent tubes are made which have increased output at the ultra-violet end of the spectrum: these are described on page 31. My experience has been that the natural-spectrum type of tubes produce a satisfactory amount of ultra-violet for amphibians. This also appears to be a logical assumption since amphibians rarely bask in the same way as does a lizard, for instance. Species may vary in their requirements, however.

In summary, a satisfactory regime for a group of breeding amphibians would consist of the following elements:

- Daily feeding with as wide a variety of live food (purchased and collected) as possible.
- Each feed should be supplemented by lightly dusting the items with a supplement which contains a high proportion of calcium.
- Lighting for the vivarium should include at least one natural-spectrum fluorescent tube which produces some light in the ultra-violet waveband.

FEEDING TADPOLES

Tadpoles usually have dietary requirements which differ greatly from those of their adult counterparts. Most frog and toad larvae are herbivorous, feeding on algae and bacteria, later graduating to tougher plant material such as the leaves of aquatic vegetation. Some species of frogs, and all newt and salamander larvae, are predatory, feeding on small aquatic invertebrates – and on each other, given the chance.

Herbivorous tadpoles may be catered for in a variety of ways. Traditionally, tadpoles were fed on green leaves such as lettuce and nettles. For newly hatched larvae these require boiling for a few minutes in order to soften them. Alternatively, natural food in the form of algae can be provided, although it is difficult to maintain a supply of this unless the tadpoles are housed outside or in a greenhouse or conservatory. Many artificial foods have been formulated, the recipes for some of these being extremely complex. Most breeders, however, have had good success with flaked fish food, easily obtainable through aquarium shops. A good-quality product should be used as this will be less likely to foul the water, and it is probably wise to use more than one brand alternately so that there is less chance of any dietary deficiency developing. Some fish flakes have colour additives, intended to make tropical fish glow like beacons: these may be useful in rearing the tadpoles of species which do not colour up well in captivity, such as the fire-bellied and yellow-bellied toads. There is plenty of scope here for experimentation.

Predatory tadpoles, of certain frogs and all salamanders, must be given very small aquatic invertebrates when they first hatch. Infusoria is often recommended: it consists of a culture of microscopic invertebrates found in natural bodies of water. Recipes for producing large quantities of infusoria rarely work in my experience, but replenishing a proportion of the water in the aquarium with sieved pondwater will undoubtedly help to maintain a small population of such creatures. Naturally there is a danger of introducing parasites, especially if the pond concerned already has a population of amphibians.

In the absence of infusoria, brine shrimp (*Artemia*) can be hatched from eggs obtained from an aquarists' supplier. These dried eggs will hatch into tiny larvae, or nauplii, in twenty-four to forty-eight hours if they are placed in a bottle of salt water and vigorously aerated. Full instructions come with the eggs. Before feeding them to the amphibians, sieve them to remove as much salt as possible – a tea-strainer is the ideal instrument for this.

Once the tadpoles begin to grow they will tackle larger prey. *Daphnia* can usually be purchased or collected locally, and if they are poured through a net the smallest individuals will end up in the aquarium while the larger ones can be returned to a container of rain water to produce more young. Eventually the tadpoles will be able to take all sizes. Larger tadpoles have a much wider range of acceptable prey, including whiteworms, *Tubifex*, small earthworms and aquatic crustaceans such as freshwater shrimps, *Gammarus*.

CHAPTER 7

Breeding

Breeding has never been as popular an aspect of the care of amphibians as it has been, for instance, with the various groups of reptiles. There are probably several reasons for this, the main one being the elaborate and costly set-ups required to persuade amphibians even to think about reproduction. Because they are traditionally inexpensive to buy, there is some resistance to spending many times the original purchase price in order to house them satisfactorily. This attitude is beginning to change at last and, as a result, a greater number of people are now breeding a greater selection of amphibian species.

Captive-bred frogs of several species are now readily available in reasonably large quantities. Several of these are rare in the wild and would not otherwise be obtained. Because of the large amount of time involved in breeding and rearing amphibians the captive-bred juveniles tend to be expensive, but they are far better adapted to captivity than wild-caught animals, less likely to be carrying diseases and parasites and usually give a far more even sex ratio. These points are in addition to the moral issue of supporting the trade in wild animals. Despite the initial cost of captive-bred stock, they are, in the long run, a better proposition and should be preferred wherever possible. Where captive-bred stock of a particular species is not available, then obviously it will be necessary to purchase wild-caught animals. This should be done, however, only when enough experience has been gained to keep them alive and when the intention is to breed from them.

Several reproductive strategies can be recognized throughout the amphibian order. Temperate species usually breed in the spring, giving their larvae the longest possible period of time to hatch, develop and metamorphose before winter stops further activity. Semi-tropical and tropical species, however, may breed repeatedly throughout the wet season, laying several batches of eggs in a single year. Aside from these basic strategies, there are a number of stimuli which may encourage amphibians to breed. A good example is that of the spadefoot toads, *Scaphiopus*, which live in arid regions and breed in response to heavy rainfall, irrespective of the time of year (but bearing in mind that the rainfall itself may be more or less seasonal). Other species are also stimulated by rainfall, especially after a short, dry spell, although not so dramatically.

Attempts to encourage captive amphibians to breed will be dependent on the species, therefore. Although many come into breeding condition in the spring, as a result of longer days or higher temperatures (or both), others require more subtle treatment. Where these parameters are known, they are given in the appropriate species accounts elsewhere in this book.

SEX DETERMINATION

Although differences between the sexes vary with species, some general points can be made. Note, though, that immature animals can be almost impossible to sex: most of the differences are due to secondary sex characteristics which develop along with sexual maturity. Furthermore, some characteristics are noticeable only during the breeding season and if the animals are in good health and well fed. Where there

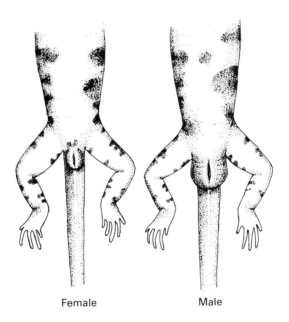

Female   Male

Fig. 5.   The most reliable difference between male and female newts and salamanders is the swollen area around the cloaca found in males. This, however, can be difficult to distinguish outside the breeding season.

is no discernible difference between individuals, such as within a group of juveniles, the only strategy is to purchase as many as can be comfortably accommodated (or afforded), grow them to maturity and hope that there will be some of each sex present. Batches of wild-caught amphibians are often heavily biased towards males because they stay around the breeding ponds longer and are easier to find in large numbers, and because tracking down their calls makes them easier to collect. Females of especially secretive species – the Asian horned frog, *Megophrys nasuta*, being one that springs readily to mind – are hardly ever seen in captivity. On the other hand, there is no evidence to suggest that captive-bred individuals are similarly biased and, in all species studied so far, the sexes are produced in equal numbers.

As a general rule the following points should be looked for when the sex of a specimen is being determined. Where differences are subtle, it is helpful to look at several individuals before a decision can be made with any degree of accuracy.

Male newts and salamanders have swollen cloacal margins and are usually more slender in general build than females of the same species. Aquatic forms often develop dorsal and caudal crests or ridges during the breeding season and, in some species, their feet may become more extensively webbed. Females become noticeably swollen immediately prior to the breeding season.

Male frogs and toads are often smaller than females – this is not much help when you are faced with a selection of half-grown individuals of equal size, however. Males of those species which breed in water usually develop some form of nuptial pad on their fore-limbs,

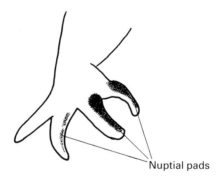

Nuptial pads

Fig. 6. Male frogs and toads usually develop nuptial pads during the breeding season. Their position varies according to the species, but they should be looked for on the inside surface of the front legs and digits. Out of the breeding season they may still be distinguishable although less obvious.

24. Palmate newt, *Triturus palmatus* (male). Male newts can often be recognized in the breeding season by their more swollen cloaca, and by secondary characteristics such as the development of a crest on tail and body (see also photographs 36 and 38) and webbing between the digits.

often on the inside surfaces of one or more digits, during the breeding season: these may still be visible, though not so obvious, throughout the year. Males of those species which call often have wrinkled and pigmented throats, either grey or yellowish, when the vocal sac is deflated.

CONDITIONING

Like all animals, amphibians will breed successfully only if they are in good health. Freshly imported animals, for instance, are usually thin and may also be dehydrated. A period of regular feeding with the appropriate diet will be necessary before there is any hope of breeding them. When adequate food is given, females will normally become plump with developing eggs. Once this occurs, the next step is to find the 'trigger' which will induce the males to start calling and the females to deposit their eggs.

25.   In many species of frog, such as *Polypedates leucomystax*, the females are appreciably larger than the males. This pair is in the process of building a foam nest for their eggs.

Creating a 'rain chamber'

One technique which is often used to encourage calling and spawning in frogs is the use of a specially constructed 'rain chamber'. There are several approaches. If the animals are kept in a large, planted set-up, for instance, with a circulation pump and appropriate pipework, they can be left where they are and only the regime needs to be manipulated. A sprinkler bar should be fitted to the outlet of the pump in such a way that the whole of the cage receives spray. The pump is operated manually, or via a time-switch, to come on for an hour or two in the early morning and again in the evening. After several days of this routine, males should start to call and the females, assuming they are well conditioned, should be prepared to release their eggs. A more simple way of inducing artificial rain is to make a special chamber, which need not be elaborate. The basis of the equipment is a plastic container of a suitable size – this may range from a small food container to a dustbin. A series of holes is drilled at an appropriate distance from the base to act as an overflow: this distance will vary with the species of frog and it is important to remember that some are not good swimmers. Water is sprayed into the container through a hosepipe fitted with a sprinkler bar or a shower head. Mains water can be used, but a closed system using dechlorinated water is better. As the water overflows through the drilled holes it can be collected in a larger plastic container and pumped back through the system. Again, two or more 'rainstorms' should be arranged each day, each lasting at least one hour. This useful technique could probably be applied equally effectively with some species of salamander.

COURTSHIP

Males of nearly all species of frog and toad call in order to attract a female. Females which are ripe will approach a calling male and signal their readiness to lay. Male attraction in newts and salamanders is less understood but is probably connected to the release of chemicals known as pheromones. Even if the animals are ready to breed and initiate courtship, no eggs will result unless the correct conditions are available for egg laying. These vary according to the species but, in the majority of cases, will include an area of water.

26.   Oak toad, *Bufo quercicus*, calling. Male frogs and toads nearly always call in order to attact a mate. The sounds produced vary according to the species, some being more melodic than others.

EGGS AND EGG LAYING

The eggs of frogs and toads are, with one or two rare exceptions, fertilized after they leave the body of the female. Newts and salamanders, on the other hand, usually practice internal fertilization in which a small packet of sperm, the spermatophore, is passed from the male to the female some hours, or days, before the fertilized eggs are laid.

Eggs may be laid singly, or in large masses or strings numbering up to several thousand eggs. The eggs or egg masses float at the surface of the water (as in the European common frog, for instance), sink to the bottom or may be attached to stones, aquatic vegetation and so on.

Species which breed in this way are quite easily catered for in captivity. They should be given an area of clean, dechlorinated water of the appropriate depth. For some species, like the clawed frogs, *Xenopus*,

this is *all* that is needed, but others require a layer of stones on the
bottom and some dead twigs and/or aquatic vegetation to which to
attach their eggs. Species that spawn among vegetation seem to prefer
fine-leaved aquatic plants and the aquatic moss *Vesicularia dubyana* has
been found to be especially useful for small species. Newts of the
genus *Triturus* like to attach their eggs singly to the leaves of aquatic
plants such as those of the pondweeds, *Elodea* species, of which a
good-sized bunch should be placed in the water. Alternatively, good
results have been obtained by partially shredding black polythene into
narrow strips, attached along one side and weighted down. Whether
the egg-laying medium is natural or artificial though, eggs should be
harvested regularly by removal of the plant or polythene every one or
two days and its replacement with fresh material. Newts may lay their
quota of eggs over a period of several days, or even weeks, and a closer
watch can be kept on the development of the eggs and young if they are
housed in batches of similar ages. If there is felt to be a danger of the
adults eating their own eggs (this applies mostly to aquatic and semi-
aquatic species such as *Xenopus*), a grid of plastic mesh should be fixed
a few centimetres from the bottom of the tank, to allow the eggs to fall
out of reach of the adults.

Frogs, toads and salamanders belonging to several distinct families
lay their eggs on the land, usually in a damp place, and development

27.   The eggs of newts and salamanders are usually laid singly or in small clumps
and are often attached to plants or stones.

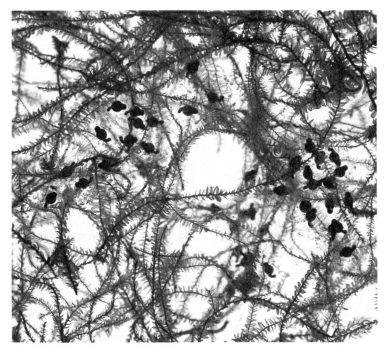

28.   The eggs of *Hyperolius marmoratus* are laid in small clumps among aquatic vegetation – Java moss is an ideal substrate for spawning this and similar species.

29.   Young tadpoles (from the clutch in photograph 28) are being accommodated here in a small plastic food container along with the clump of Java moss in which they were laid.

30. Some species depart from the more usual habit of depositing their eggs in water and lay small clutches in a damp place on land. In the case of these *Mantella aurantiaca* eggs, the resultant tadpoles will wriggle to water and continue their development in the normal way. Other species complete their entire development within the egg capsule and are thus independent of open water.

begins out of the water. There is even variation here, however. A number of frog species, such as the pyllomedusine tree frogs (page 170), attach their clutches to vegetation overhanging water, so that the newly hatched larvae drop into the water once they have hatched. Others guard the eggs until they hatch and then move the tadpoles to water, whereas yet others carry the eggs by a variety of means, releasing them into the water when they have hatched or, sometimes, retaining them until they have completed their development. Quite a large number of frogs lay eggs beneath logs or in damp moss and the entire development takes place within the egg membrane. Amphibians of this type should be permanently housed in cages with a damp mossy substrate and pieces of bark and logs under which they can lay their eggs. See the species account of *Eleutherodactylus johnstonei* (page 153) for more details.

Salamanders can be equally inventive and, although most lay their eggs in water, some deposit them on the land while others retain them within their body until they have grown into well-developed tadpoles or, in one case, into fully formed young salamanders. It is obviously important to establish the life-cycle of the species concerned before any attempt can be made to breed it.

DEVELOPMENT

Typical amphibian eggs are covered with several layers of gelatinous material. This protects them from attack by fungi and, in species which lay their eggs out of the water, from desiccation. The egg itself is usually black on top and white or grey below, parts known respectively as the animal pole and the vegetal pole. As the embryo develops, the animal pole extends around the vegetal pole until it encloses it completely. Shortly after this the egg loses its rounded shape and the larva begins to take form. Eventually the larvae break free of the egg membrane and become independent.

Catering for aquatic amphibian larvae is more akin to fish keeping than to amphibian keeping. It is especially important to pay attention to details such as water quality (see Chapter 3) and feeding. As a rule tadpoles fare better in large, well-planted aquaria than in small sterile containers. Apart from other factors, water quality is less prone to sudden changes in large containers, while the presence of healthy plant life will also act to some extent as a buffer against fluctuations in the levels of dissolved gases and so on. Light is also of great importance. Most tadpoles seem to do better under a fairly strong light, and natural light is preferable to artificial light. Again there is an interplay with other factors here – plants will grow and photosynthesize better under strong light and will therefore be working more effectively to maintain water quality. There are exceptions, though and these are noted in the individual species accounts later in the book.

Most salamander tadpoles, and some frog and toad tadpoles, are predatory. Where they are kept in large batches there is always a danger of intra-specific predation: in other words, cannibalism. With prolific species this is not necessarily a bad thing since it will be the smaller and weaker individuals which will be eaten, allowing a limited degree of natural selection to occur. With those species which lay only a few eggs, however, each larvae is precious and it is obviously more important to rear as many as possible. Rearing species of this type may require a more elaborate set-up and some suggestions are given in the chapter on poison-dart frogs, which are a case in point.

As the larvae begin to metamorphose, their requirements change and, in particular, it may be advantageous to provide ultra-violet light in the form of one of the natural-spectrum fluorescent tubes (see pages 30 and 68). Although some species are good climbers and will merely walk up the side of the aquarium (which will therefore need to be well covered), others seem able neither to climb nor swim well once they have metamorphosed. Here it will be essential to allow them easy

31.   A tree frog tadpole nearing metamorphosis. This stage brings about many behavioural and physiological changes to the animal and correct conditions are very important.

access to terra firma by placing several floating 'islands' of cork or polystyrene on the water's surface, for instance, or by lowering the water level and tilting the aquarium slightly to form a sloping 'shore'.

Aquatic species, of course, need no special arrangements to be made for their metamorphosis; they can simply be left in the same aquarium. This also applies to some species of newts which, given the chance, will leave the water as efts but which are much easier to feed and accommodate if they are not given the chance to do so. These species do not have an obligatory terrestrial phase (except, perhaps, as hibernating adults) and are equally capable of living totally aquatic lives.

Newly metamorphosed froglets should be transferred to smaller versions of the accommodation used for the adults and fed on appropriately sized insects. Once they have begun to feed and grow well they can be treated in the same way as the adults.

HORMONE-INDUCED BREEDING

The use of hormones to induce reproduction in amphibians, especially the more commercially important frogs and toads, is now becoming more common. The techniques involved, though not difficult to acquire, are beyond the scope of this book, while some of the equipment and the hormones themselves are not freely available. For the interest of readers a brief account of the principles is given.

First, it must be stressed that the animals used must be in good

32. Horned frogs 'do it with hormones'!

breeding condition. Hormones cannot stimulate females to develop eggs over a period of a few days but only to release eggs which have been formulated but which, for some reason or other, they refuse to lay, usually because some environmental stimulus is lacking.

Second, it should be pointed out that the hormones used are naturally occurring chemicals which, in the normal course of events, would be produced by the pituitary gland, or associated glands, of the frogs. Using hormones to induce breeding is merely a way of duplicating a natural process.

A variety of hormones have been found to be effective. They may be of a type which work directly on the reproductive organs of the animals: that is, gonadotropins, including HCG (human chorionic gonadotropin), which was widely used to induce spawning in the clawed frog, *Xenopus laevis*, before chemical means of pregnancy testing were available. Alternatively hormones which stimulate the pituitary into manufacturing gonadotropins may be used, sometimes with greater effect. The most common of these is luteinizing hormone-releasing hormone (LHRH); in other words, it is a hormone which stimulates the pituitary gland to release a second hormone. This is sometimes known as a 'cascade' effect.

Both males and females are usually given a dose of the chosen hormone, invariably by injection. Males do not require such a high dose because they are, biologically, always in a state of readiness or near-readiness to breed, whereas females require more stimulation. Males usually require one tenth to one half of the female dose. The actual dose rate varies with the hormone used, and sometimes, a smaller 'primer' injection is given to females about three or four days before the main one.

As soon as the main dose is given to both sexes, they are placed together in an appropriate container of water so that spawning can take place. This may occur from a few hours to two days later. The adults are returned to their cage and the eggs are collected and reared in the normal way. Offspring resulting from hormonally induced spawnings are indistinguishable from other larvae of the same species and are capable of breeding, either naturally or, in their turn, by means of hormone injections.

Species which have been bred in this way include clawed frogs, *Xenopus* species; horned frogs, *Ceratophrys* species; Budgett's frog and its relatives, *Lepidobatrachus* species; White's tree frogs, *Litoria caerulea*; Australian bullfrogs, *Cyclorana* species; Cane toads, *Bufo marinus*; and a number of endangered species such as the American *Bufo houstonensis*.

CHAPTER 8

Management and Health

Although amphibians are susceptible to a range of diseases and afflictions, very little is known about their control. Taking a sick newt to the local vet is unlikely to result in a cure or even very much sympathy.

On the other hand, the vast majority of problems are likely to be caused by the poor conditions under which amphibians are housed, or under which they were kept prior to purchase. Incorrect temperatures, poor water quality and physical injuries result in stress even where they do not kill outright and very often recovery is slow even if the animal is given the best attention. Some species are highly specialized in ways which are not well understood and rarely live more than a few weeks in captivity however much trouble is taken with their care. These species are either not listed in this book or warnings are given under their descriptions.

Because amphibians are in close association with their immediate environment, they are more sensitive to chemical pollution and over-crowding than other animals. Water quality is dealt with elsewhere but it is worth emphasizing here that frogs and salamanders secrete small quantities of toxic chemicals from specialized glands and from their skins. These can quickly build up in small bodies of water, such as are contained in water bowls, leading to pollution of the water and self-poisoning. Frequent water changes are the easy answer to this problem. Mechanical aids such as filters and organic remedies such as a healthy and vigorous plant growth will also go a long way towards avoiding trouble with aquatic species or larvae.

Additional precautions relate to chemicals and materials used for cleaning out cages, and for handling and holding the animals. All nets, buckets, containers, water bowls and so on should be kept free of powerful cleaning materials and disinfectants. Ideally they should be used specially for the amphibians rather than impounded from the garden, kitchen or bathroom. If rain water is to be used for tadpoles and aquatic and semi-aquatic species, it should be collected and stored in clean glass or plastic containers used for nothing else (and so labelled). Should a serious infection break out it may be necessary to disinfect some cages and items of equipment, but cheap items, such as nets, rocks and other cage furnishings, should be discarded and replaced with new. Finally, great care must be taken when using pesticides, insecticides and other '-cides' in the vicinity of amphibian cages, either indoors or out. In particular, insects from an area which has been recently sprayed should on no account be fed to amphibians, whatever assurances are given on the container.

Dietary deficiencies often occur over an extended period and may not be noticed until the animals are so badly malnourished that correction is difficult. Look out for weak jaws and poorly developed hind-limbs, especially in young animals: if a few individuals in a group of youngsters show signs of deficiency, assume that they are all suffering and treat accordingly, either by increasing their dietary vitamin supplement or by providing a source of ultra-violet light (see page 31). Lack of colour is often associated with captive-bred frogs and may be connected to diet. Species which are grass-green in the wild are often bluish-green or even greyish when raised in captivity but are otherwise normal. White's tree frog, *Litoria caerulea*, is an example of a species in which this condition is often seen. There seems to be no way to counteract this at the time of writing, but cautious experimentation with diet and/or lighting may provide an answer. Brightly coloured species such as the yellow and fire-bellied toads, *Bombina*, will fail to develop their bright ventral coloration unless fed extracts of naturally occurring pigments: this is dealt with under their species accounts. Chapter 6 provides additional guidelines which should be followed in the absence of more specific information about the particular species concerned.

Injuries can occur from fighting or rough handling or they may be self-inflicted. Overcrowded and/or underfed larvae often chew pieces from one another and, although lost limbs will usually regenerate before metamorphosis, secondary infections can occur. Avoiding the conditions which led to the behaviour is the best cure, while badly damaged animals should be isolated and treated with anti-fungal solutions to avoid further trouble. Although there are many antibiotics available, older cures are often just as effective, are easier to obtain and may be safer to use. Methylene blue and malachite green solutions can be obtained from aquarists' suppliers and used at the recommended rate for larvae and twice the recommended rate for adults of aquatic species. Higher dosages are also helpful in the case of persistent fungal infections, but caution should be used when treating delicate or valuable animals. Note also that aquatic plants are killed when concentrated solutions of either of the above chemicals are used. There are several ways of treating injuries to terrestrial amphibians. Commercial solution (3 per cent) hydrogen peroxide or an iodine solution such as Betadine may be applied to the injury with a small paint brush. Alternatively, the area may be dusted with an antibiotic powder such as Cicatrin which has been found effective in curing fire salamanders with necrotic toes. Again, caution must be used when dealing with these substances.

So-called 'red-leg disease' in frogs may be caused by an *Aeromonas* infection, but in newly imported animals is more likely to be the result of abrasions caused by a dry substrate such as cardboard. In the latter case no treatment is necessary except to correct the cause as soon as possible and to keep the animal(s) in scrupulously clean cages for a few days. Red-leg caused by bacteria can sometimes be cleared up by housing the frogs in chlorinated water – that is, tap water – for a few days. Terramycin can also be effective but should be administered only under the supervision of a veterinary surgeon.

Imported animals are sometimes infested with ecto- and endo-parasites such as leeches, flukes and parasitic worms. Visible parasites can be removed with a pair of forceps but internal ones are more difficult to detect and eradicate. Very often the parasites require some intermediate host to complete their life-cycle, and when the animals are in a hygienic environment re-infestation cannot occur. The parasite burden is then gradually reduced without any form of treatment.

With the exception of some of the more specific problems mentioned above, keeping amphibians fit and healthy depends more than anything else on the ability to spot abnormal behaviour, assess the causes and correct the conditions before it is too late.

PART II

Caecilians, Newts and Salamanders

CHAPTER 9

Caecilians

The caecilians are a little-studied group of amphibians with no common name. There are about 160 species, all found in tropical regions. Some are aquatic or semi-aquatic, while others live in damp soil and leaf-litter beneath stones and logs or in burrows. They look more like earthworms than amphibians, having elongated bodies with segmented rings around them. Their eyes are small and may be covered by skin, but they have large mouths. Some are attractively coloured.

Very few species have been kept in captivity. In all honesty their secretive habits exclude them from consideration by all but the most dedicated enthusiasts, but there is an element of challenge in finding the right conditions for them and, since almost nothing is known about their reproductive habits, amateurs could make important observations. In nature, caecilians have diverse reproductive systems. About half the known species apparently give birth to live young. Of the egg-laying species, some have typical amphibian life-cycles with a larval form, whereas others (all terrestrial) have direct development whereby the young hatch, fully formed, from eggs laid in underground chambers.

AQUATIC SPECIES

Most of the caecilians which turn up in Europe and North America are included, by accident, with shipments of tropical fish from various parts of the world. It follows, then, that they will usually be of the aquatic types. At least three species have been seen in Europe in recent years, but their exact identification is often difficult to ascertain. Treating these in the same way as other aquatic amphibians has kept them alive successfully. They should have a large aquarium, half-filled with soft water, preferably rain water. Frequent water changes are advisable as caecilians may produce toxins from the skin. The aquarium should have a substrate of fine gravel or soil and hiding places in the form of driftwood, flowerpots and so on should be provided. It should also be

33. South American caecilian, *Siphonops annulata*. This is one of the more terrestrial species which requires rather specialized accommodation.

thickly planted with Java moss or a similar species and floating plants such as *Salvinia* should be used to filter the light. Rooted plants will not last very long because of constant disturbance by the caecilians. A temperature of 25°C should be maintained by means of an aquarium heater and the lighting should be subdued. A range of live food should be offered: prey which has been successfully used to feed these amphibians includes small goldfish and earthworms.

There is only one account of captive breeding. A group of *Typhlonectes compressicauda*, from Brazil, was kept in an aquarium which was subject to small fluctuations in temperature. Mating was observed in the autumn and the females gave birth to three to seven live young after a gestation period of five to seven months. The young have external gills which are shed soon after birth.

TERRESTRIAL SPECIES

Very little is known about the long-term requirements of terrestrial caecilians. A single specimen of *Siphonops annulatus* was kept for several months in a vivarium with a deep layer of damp leaf-litter and sphagnum moss. A temperature of about 25°C was maintained by means of an underfloor heat-pad and earthworms were introduced as food – although the caecilian was never seen to eat, the earthworms gradually disappeared at the rate of about one each week. There is no information on captive reproduction in this or in any of the other terrestrial caecilians.

CHAPTER 10

Cryptobranchidae: Giant Salamanders

The primitive family Cryptobranchidae contains only three species, the two giant salamanders of Japan and China, *Andrias japonicus* and *A. davidianus*, and the North American hellbender, *Cryptobranchus alleganiensis*.

The Asian species, which may grow to over 1.5 m, are both endangered and protected. The American species is smaller, growing to 60 cm, and, although quite numerous where it occurs, is rarely offered in the pet trade. They are magnificent amphibians, but rather grotesque in appearance with folds of wrinkled skin running along their bodies and huge, flattened heads. All are voracious predators on fish and large aquatic invertebrates such as crayfish.

All three species are found in clear, flowing streams and rivers in montane regions, where they lead secretive lives beneath rocks and debris. In captivity, should they ever become available, it would be necessary to go to great lengths to provide suitable accommodation, the main requirement being well-oxygenated, clear water and an ample diet of fish. Their tanks must be well covered otherwise they are inclined to climb out and wander off across country. Although they have a robust constitution, they sometimes suffer from the usual fungal diseases associated with many aquatic amphibians: a satisfactory environment is the best way of avoiding these.

In contrast to most salamanders, fertilization in these species is external. The male hellbender, for instance, scoops out a nest in gravel and encourages females to enter and lay their eggs, which he then fertilizes. Several females may subsequently lay in the same nest. The eggs are guarded by the male throughout their long development, which takes ten to twelve weeks. The larvae are about 3 cm long when they hatch and retain their external gills for eighteen months, by which time they measure about 12 cm.

CHAPTER 11

Salamandridae: Newts, Fire Salamanders and Related Species

The family Salamandridae contains over fifty species distributed throughout Europe and parts of North America and South-east Asia. It is a diverse family, including totally aquatic as well as totally terrestrial species, but most are terrestrial except during the breeding season when they spend varying amounts of time in ponds and slow-moving streams. A number of species are popular subjects for vivaria and several are well suited to outdoor enclosures.

1: NEWTS

'Newt' is a rather vague term for the species which enter ponds to breed in the spring then spend varying amounts of time living aquatically until they leave the water again at some time in the summer. During the aquatic phase the males often develop fins and webbing on their feet to enable them to swim more efficiently after females. The rest of the year, including a period of hibernation, is spent in damp areas on land (where they are rarely seen). With a few exceptions these species seem to do best if they spend at least part of the year outside, in a pond, large aquarium or an enclosure such as a greenhouse or coldframe. In this way they will come into breeding condition naturally and spawning will usually take place with little additional stimulation.

In their aquatic phase all species are fairly easily catered for. They are not particularly demanding regarding temperature and most will happily tolerate a range of, say, between 5° and 20°C. They require an abundant supply of live food, including earthworms and smaller invertebrates such as *Tubifex*, *Daphnia* and whiteworms, all of which are readily available from aquarists' suppliers. Alternatively, a local pond can be netted occasionally, producing a wide range of food species. Note that newts are voracious predators of frog and toad tadpoles, seemingly preferring these above all other food. They are therefore definitely unsuitable for enclosures containing breeding colonies of any of these species.

All species of newt breed in spring, in response to rising temperature and lengthening days. If they are kept in an outdoor enclosure with a pool they will make their own way into the water when they are ready. Otherwise they should be placed in an aquarium at this time. Fertilization is usually external, with the male depositing a small package of sperm, the spermatophore, on the substrate and then encouraging the female, by means of an elaborate courtship 'dance', to move forward until she is in a position to take it up into her cloaca. Spawning usually begins a day or two later and may continue for a week or more. The eggs are usually laid singly, each being carefully placed on the leaf of an aquatic plant which is then folded over it. For newts in captivity shredded black polythene can be used as a substitute for plants (see page 77), and the batches of eggs removed regularly to be hatched in a separate aquarium or pond. The larvae require plenty of small live food, starting with zooplankton, best obtained by sieving natural pond water. They soon graduate to newly hatched brine shrimp and small *Daphnia*, after which providing enough food for them becomes easier. As they grow they will require separating into batches of similar-sized young, as a measure against cannibalism, and frequent water changes are recommended to prevent the build-up of toxins from uneaten food and from the larvae themselves.

When the larvae metamorphose they have a compulsion to leave the water. They can be helped in this if a heap of pebbles is placed in the aquarium, just breaking the surface. The aquarium should be inspected once or twice each day and any small newts removed to separate rearing containers, or released into a suitable outdoor enclosure. Although the young of some species will continue to live aquatically if forced to do so, others may be reared in a terrestrial environment. They can be kept on a substrate of moist peat, leaves, sphagnum moss or damp paper towels with several small pieces of bark or shards of clay flower pots under which they can hide. The container should have a lid as young newts are good at scaling smooth surfaces. They will eat most small invertebrates provided they are not too quick to be caught. *Tubifex*, which can be placed in a shallow dish within the container, or whiteworms can be used as staple foods, although the young newts will grow more rapidly if a variety of species is offered.

As sexual maturity is reached, usually at one or two years of age, the newts should be allowed to become cool during the winter and then placed in an aquatic set-up in the spring. This will stimulate the females to develop eggs and the males to develop the fins, crests and other secondary sex characteristics associated with reproduction.

Japanese fire-bellied newt, *Cynops pyrrhogaster*

The Japanese fire-bellied newt grows to about 15 cm in length. It is dark brown, almost black in colour, with a startling reddish-orange underside. There may be a few isolated black blotches within the orange area.

This species does very well in captivity. Although it will voluntarily leave the water at the end of the breeding season, it is best treated as an aquatic species. It should be given a large aquarium with at least 20 cm of water. This should be thickly planted with species such as *Elodea*, and one or two large rocks or pieces of driftwood should project just above the water's surface. It is undemanding in its temperature requirements but should not be kept too warm: room temperature in an east- or west-facing window is usually satisfactory throughout the year. Alternatively, light can be provided with natural-spectrum fluorescent tubes, but you should make sure that there is adequate light for healthy

34. Japanese fire-bellied newt, *Cynops pyrrhogaster*, an attractive and interesting species for the aquatic or semi-aquatic vivarium.

35. Paddle-tailed newt, *Cynops ensicauda*, a more unusual species than
C. pyrrhogaster and one about which little is known.

plant growth. During the summer the aquarium can be moved outside
or the newts transferred to an outside aquarium or small pond. This
species will eat most aquatic invertebrates such as *Daphnia* and *Tubifex*,
as well as earthworms.

Breeding takes place in the spring and is more likely to be successful
if the newts have been kept cool (down to 5°C) during the winter.
Following an elaborate courtship the female picks up a packet of sperm
deposited by the male and begins to lay her eggs a day or two later.
Each egg is stuck to the leaf of an aquatic plant, which is then folded
over the egg. If it is hoped to rear a large number of young, bunches of
plants should be removed every two days and replaced with fresh
material, otherwise the larvae may get eaten by the adults when they
hatch. Rearing can be carried out using the system described on page
93. The larvae metamorphose by the end of their first summer, the
exact time depending on food supply and, more importantly, temperature. They can be returned to an aquatic environment the following
spring where they will remain for the rest of their lives.

SIMILAR SPECIES

The paddle-tailed newt, *Cynops ensicauda*, is from Japan. It is longer than *C. pyrrhogaster* with smooth, slimy skin and has less orange beneath. The tail is long and greatly flattened from side to side. It can be kept in the same way as *C. pyrrhogaster* but is probably not so hardy.

The Hong Kong fire-bellied newt *Paramesotriton hongkongensis* is sometimes imported. This looks very similar to the above two species but has a crimson underside and smoother skin. For some unknown reason it does not do nearly so well in captivity and is best avoided.

Red-spotted newt, *Notophthalmus viridescens*

The red-spotted newt is quite common, being found throughout the eastern half of North America, where a number of subspecies are recognized. It grows to a maximum of 10 cm in length and is olive-green in colour, with a paler, often yellowish underside. Small red spots are scattered over the back and flanks. The male develops a low crest above and below his tail during the breeding season, along with rough black areas on his hind-limbs and feet. The young are totally unlike the adults, being orange or red all over. This is the terrestrial stage, during which they are known as 'red efts'.

Care and breeding are as described on page 93. The efts are terrestrial: once the coloration of the juveniles changes to that of the adult form they can be returned permanently to an aquarium.

Ribbed newt (or ribbed salamander), *Pleurodeles waltl*

The ribbed newt is an interesting species from southern Spain and North-west Africa. Brown in colour with some darker mottlings, it has a flattened, toad-like head. It gets its common name from its ribs, which have sharp ends and sometimes pierce the skin in old individuals, forming two rows of spines on either side of the backbone: this is presumably a means of defence.

It is most easily kept in a permanently aquatic set-up. It requires about 30 cm of water at 20-25°C in summer, about 10°C in winter. The substrate should be gravel or sand, decorated with pieces of drift-wood and robust aquatic plants. Floating plants such as *Salvinia* will help to diffuse the light as well as looking attractive. Food is no problem: this species will eat most aquatic invertebrates, earthworms and strips of lean meat.

Breeding occurs in the spring but may extend through the summer. Amplexus takes place under water and the spermatophore is deposited on the substrate before being taken up by the female. Egg laying may then be delayed for several weeks. The eggs are laid in small groups, attached to plants, wood or stones, and can number up to 1000. They hatch after about one week and are easily reared in the usual way.

Rough-skinned newt, *Taricha granulosa*

The rough-skinned newt and two similar but rarely seen relatives are robust species from western North America. They are dark brown above and orange below. During the terrestrial phase the skin of *T. granulosa* becomes rough as a result of the development of many small tubercles scattered over the surface.

A warmer temperature is appreciated by the rough-skinned newt, about 20°C being satisfactory, although it needs to be cooled down slightly over the winter if it is to breed successfully. Breeding males have patches of rugose, dark skin on the palms of their fore- and hind-limbs. The eggs are laid singly and the larvae and juveniles should be reared as described on page 93.

SIMILAR SPECIES
The other two species in the genus are *Taricha tortosa*, the Californian newt, and *T. rivularis*, the red-bellied newt (not to be confused with the Japanese species with a similar name). Their care and breeding is as above, but both these species lay their eggs in small clumps.

Alpine newt, *Triturus alpestris*

The European alpine newt is found in cold ponds, streams and lakes in northern, central and southern Europe. In the south it is restricted to montane areas, and in Spain an isolated population, *Triturus alpestris cyreni*, is found high up in the Cantabrian Mountains. The species grows to just over 10 cm; the Spanish subspecies is slightly smaller. This beautiful newt is intricately marked. The back is almost black, though the colour becomes lighter on the flanks. The underside is orange in males, yellowish in females. Small, dark spots are present along the flanks and the tail. The flanks and tail of the male acquire a violet sheen during the breeding season and they grow a low crest barred with black and pale yellow.

Care and breeding are as described on page 93. As may be expected, this species is very cold-tolerant and will live and breed readily in an outdoor pond. It has become naturalized outside its natural range in several parts of northern Europe.

97

Crested newt, *Triturus cristatus*

The crested newt is the largest species of *Triturus*, with some animals approaching 20 cm in length. It is found throughout most of Europe, except in the Iberian peninsula and parts of western France. The warty skin is dark brown or black above with a bright orange underside. The throat and flanks are speckled with small, pearly-white warts. Breeding males develop a high, ragged crest and a bluish-white stripe along each side of the tail.

Care and breeding are described on page 93. This newt is easily naturalized in a large garden pond with plenty of aquatic vegetation and ample cover around the margins. Wild populations of the species are protected over much of its range, including Great Britain.

SIMILAR SPECIES

The Italian crested newt, *Triturus carnifex*, was formerly regarded as a subspecies of the crested newt. It is similar in appearance but lacks the pearly warts on the flanks, and the female has a thin orange or yellow vertebral line along the back. Care and breeding are as described on page 93, but a slightly warmer temperature is required.

Marbled newt, *Triturus marmoratus*

The marbled newt is possibly the most attractive member of its genus. It grows to about the same size and proportions as the crested newt but is distinctly marked. The back and sides are marbled in bright green and black, while the underside is grey. The female has a bright orange vertebral line along the back and the top of the tail, whereas the male develops a magnificent crest of cream-and-black bars during the breeding season.

Care and breeding are as described on page 93. In nature, this species spends little time in the water, entering ponds for only a few weeks in the spring in order to breed. It will, however, adapt well to an aquatic life in an aquarium with a few emergent rocks and plenty of healthy vegetation. It is rather more delicate than the crested newt and, although it may survive in protected outdoor enclosures throughout the year, breeding animals at least should be brought indoors during the coldest parts of the winter. Alternatively it can be kept in a moderately heated greenhouse. Sunlight appears to be an important stimulus to spawning in this species.

The marbled newt and the crested newt apparently hybridize in areas where their ranges overlap. The offspring show characteristics of both species. There are no records of this occurring in captivity.

36. Male crested newt, *Triturus cristatus*, in breeding condition.

37. Juvenile European marbled newt, *Triturus marmoratus*. Females retain the orange vertebral stripe, whereas males develop a high crest during the breeding season.

Smooth newt, *Triturus vulgaris*

The smooth newt is one of several small European species which are rather similar in appearance. It grows to about 10 cm in length and is pale to dark brown in colour with a yellow to orange underside. Males are heavily spotted in dark brown and develop a high, wavy crest during the breeding season. There are some geographical variations and several subspecies are recognized.

Care and breeding are as described on page 93. This is an ideal species for naturalizing but not in ponds where frogs or toads are established as their tadpoles are greatly relished.

SIMILAR SPECIES
The palmate newt, *Triturus helveticus*, has a similar range to that of the smooth newt and can be cared for in the same way. There are also several other closely related species which have similar requirements.

38. Male smooth newt, *Triturus vulgaris*, in breeding condition. In suitable climates this species adapts well to naturalizing in garden ponds.

2: SALAMANDERS

A few members of this large family are rather more terrestrial than the newts described in Group 1. These are more commonly referred to as 'salamanders', although the distinction is rather arbitrary.

European fire salamander, *Salamandra salamandra*

The well-known and distinctive European fire salamander is deservedly popular as a vivarium subject. It is large, about 20 cm in length but exceptionally to 30 cm, stockily built and brilliantly marked in glossy black and yellow. The arrangement of the yellow markings varies within the range of the species and a number of subspecies are recognized. The more common and distinctive forms include *S. s. salamandra*, from central and eastern Europe, in which the yellow markings take the form of irregular spots and squiggles; *S. s. terrestris*, from central and northern Europe, in which they are arranged as a pair of broad dorso-lateral stripes; and *S. s. gigliolii*, from Italy, in which the yellow areas are greatly expanded, sometimes covering almost the whole of the back with only a few small incursions of black.

The care and breeding of all these forms is fundamentally the same. Indoors they require large vivaria wth a substrate of peat, leaf-litter or other damp material. Orchid compost, consisting of small chips of bark with the addition of small amounts of perlite and granulated charcoal, is a useful substitute. Hiding places, in the form of large, curved pieces of bark, or flat rocks, are essential. If a pool is provided – for example, for breeding purposes – the water must be shallow: fire salamanders are unable to swim and will drown if they become trapped in deep water. They dislike temperatures above 20°C, and so sunny situations should be avoided. On the other hand, they will happily survive temperatures down to freezing and there is thus no need to provide any supplementary heating. The cage should be sprayed regularly with water in order to keep the substrate damp. Planting is possible, especially with ferns, mosses and ivies, all of which will thrive in low light. Feeding should not present a problem. Fire salamanders will eat most small invertebrates and especially like earthworms and slugs. Crickets, waxworms and mealworms can also be offered occasionally, but all cultured food should be dusted with a vitamin and mineral preparation.

Fire salamanders are at their best, however, when kept in large outdoor enclosures. These should be situated in a shady part of the garden and, during dry weather, may require regular watering. Piles of

101

39.   One of the striped forms of the European fire salamander, *Salamandra salamandra*, from the Cantabrian Mountains in northern Spain.

40.   Italian form of the fire salamander, *Salamandra salamandra gigliolii*, in which the black markings are greatly reduced.

rock or, better still, rotting logs should be included and it is a good idea to give a surface-dressing of dead oak or beech leaves every autumn. A variety of plants can be grown in and around the enclosure. Although the inhabitants will find a certain amount of their food naturally, extra earthworms and so on should be added whenever convenient. A small, shallow pool with sloping sides could be a permanent fixture, and larvae will often be found at various times of the year. Although the salamanders are fairly secretive, it should be possible to inspect them during the evening, especially during periods of wet or damp weather, or if the enclosure is liberally watered. If they are to remain in the enclosure throughout the winter, there must obviously be some means for them to find their way into a frost-free chamber (see Chapter 4).

Mating takes place on land, usually in spring or early summer. The male chases the female until amplexus is permitted, the male lying under the female with his fore-limbs hooked around hers. Then he deposits his spermatophore, which is taken up immediately by the female. She retains the developing eggs and gives birth to well-grown larvae several months after mating; occasionally she will retain them until the following spring. Birth takes place in shallow water and a water container should be provided whenever females are suspected of being pregnant. The female backs down into the water until the lower half of her body is submerged and gives birth to up to fifty larvae. These lack the bright markings of the adults but are bronze-gold in colour. Care and rearing of the larvae follow the usual pattern, plenty of small, live invertebrates being required as food material. In the absence of sufficient food, a degree of cannibalism is inevitable and larvae will often snap at the limbs and tails of cage-mates. The bright adult coloration appears at the time of metamorphosis, when the animals should be given a sloping bank of gravel or pebbles in order to help them leave the water. The young require similar accommodation to the adults and should be fed on small earthworms, waxworms and, especially sweepings (small insects collected from the undergrowth by means of a butterfly net or sweep net). Sexual maturity takes two to four years, depending on temperature and food supply.

SIMILAR SPECIES

The alpine salamander, *Salamandra atra*, and the recently described *S. lanai*, occur in the high Alps. They lack the yellow markings and are altogether more slender in build. Their method of reproduction is even less dependent on water as the females retain the larvae until they are metamorphosed, invariably giving birth to two young. They are protected throughout their range, however, and are in any case hard to care for, needing cold, damp conditions at all times.

Mandarin salamander or crocodile newt, *Tylotriton verrucosus*

This species is one of the few Asian salamanders to be available, although only spasmodically. It occurs in western China and in adjacent parts of Indo-China. Growing to a stocky 18 cm in length, it is strikingly marked. The background colour is dark brown and the skin is rugose, unlike that of the fire salamander. There is a broad, yellowish-orange vertebral stripe beginning on the top of the head and continuing on to the tail. The large parotid glands on either side of the head are also orange and there is a row of orange nodules along either flank, marking the end of the ribs.

Although the species is often collected during its aquatic phase, it should not be kept in an aquatic environment. Its accommodation and feeding requirements are much the same as those of the fire salamander,

41.   Chinese mandarin newt, *Tylotriton verrucosus*.

but it should be kept at a somewhat higher temperature, 20-25°C being ideal for most of the year. If it is cooled down slightly during the winter, it should come into breeding condition in the spring. At this time it will require a large water container in the vivarium. Amplexus takes place in the water and fertilization is internal. The female lays about fifty eggs two weeks after mating has taken place and these are attached to the leaves of aquatic plants, which should then be removed so that the larvae can be hatched and reared separately. With adequate feeding, the larvae metamorphose four to six months later.

CHAPTER 12

Ambystomatidae: Axolotl and Mole Salamanders

The salamanders belonging to the Ambystomatidae are exclusively North American. Although there are thirty-five species altogether, few of them are widely kept in captivity. One species, however, is among the most numerous of all captive amphibians and is bred by the thousand by amateur herpetoculturalists and laboratories. This, of course, is the axolotl, *Ambystoma mexicanum*.

In many ways the mole salamanders are the American counterparts of the European *Salamandra* species and are typically found in damp, humid environments, secreting themselves by day and coming out to forage under the cover of darkness. In spring most of them repair to ponds and streams in order to reproduce and become aquatic for a while. Yet they do not develop the crests and fins which are characteristic of the more aquatic species of the Salamandridae. Many species are attractively marked and there is no reason why a greater variety of species could not be successfully kept and bred in captivity. A number of them would almost certainly adapt well to an outdoor enclosure.

Care of all the species so far attempted is similar. They require moderate temperatures: up to about 23°C in summer, cooler in winter. Humidity should be kept high by spraying but ventilation must be good: unless flying insects are used for food it may not be necessary to cover the vivarium at all. The substrate must be kept damp and a 10 cm layer of leaf-litter has been found to be ideal. On top of this can be placed a selection of large pieces of bark to provide hiding places. Plants, such as ferns and ivies, are best left in their pots, which can be buried to the rim in the substrate. Food is no problem as these species are greedy and efficient predators. They will take quite active prey, such as crickets, as well as earthworms and slugs. Some of the larger species will also accept dead newborn mice if these are dangled in front of them with forceps.

Captive breeding seems not to have been achieved with any degree of regularity, probably through lack of interest. It would undoubtedly take place as a matter of course if the salamanders were to be kept outside in a garden enclosure in a suitable climate. The larvae are predatory and should be fed on small invertebrates such as *Daphne* and *Artemia* at first, then moved on to larger items such as small earthworms.

Neotony is a fairly frequent occurrence in this family. In this state the larvae fail to metamorphose but continue to grow and mature in the larval form. The most obvious example of this may be observed in the axolotl, *Ambystoma mexicanum*, but neotonic examples of the tiger salamander, *A. tigrinum*, are also fairly frequent. Neotonic individuals should be kept in the same way as larvae (which they are!), but their food requirements will obviously be scaled up.

The axolotl will be dealt with first, followed by the terrestrial forms.

Axolotl, *Ambystoma mexicanum*

The axolotl (from an Aztec word meaning 'water monster') is found in only a few high lakes in central Mexico. As a result of environmental pollution, land drainage and other human activities, the natural population of axolotls is in dire straits: this is in strong contrast to the state of affairs among captive animals, for many thousands of axolotls are bred successfully each year by amateurs and researchers.

The axolotl may grow to 30 cm, although it usually remains somewhat smaller than this. The natural colour is dark grey but several mutations are cultured, the most common of which is an albino strain. The head is wide and the mouth large. Immediately behind the head, on each side, are three branched external gills. These gills vary in size according to the temperature at which the animal is kept, the largest developing on individuals which are kept in warm water. There are many ways in which axolotls can be kept and bred successfully, but the simplest is to keep a pair of them in an aquarium measuring about 90 cm × 45 cm × 45 cm deep. Rain water or matured aquarium water should be used; it can be kept clean by means of a small filter (power or airlift). The substrate may be coarse river sand or pea gravel and larger pebbles or stones can be used to decorate the set-up. Plants are not strictly necessary but will help to keep the water 'sweet', and suitable species include pondweed, *Elodea*, and Java moss, *Vesicularia*. Axolotls will eat maggots, earthworms and small fish; strips of lean meat may also be fed but are not ideal and should be used only occasionally or in an emergency. During spring and summer the water should be kept at

107

about 20°C; a winter cooling-off period, to 5° or 10°C, is possible and may be beneficial to breeding.

The male is recognizable by his more slender shape and swollen cloacal region. Females are plump when well fed. Spawning takes place as a result of cool conditions and can often be stimulated by a partial water change, in which water which is appreciably cooler is used to replace about half of the existing water. After a rather lacklustre display of chasing and nudging, the male deposits a spermatophore on the substrate, often on a rough stone if one is available. The female takes the spermatophore into her cloaca and spawning begins shortly afterwards. A complete clutch of eggs may number up to 500 or more in large females and they are stuck to plants, rocks or twigs or scattered over the substrate.

The eggs should be removed before the adults have time to eat them and this is best achieved by the use of a bulb pipette: they are trans-ferred to a separate aquarium or a large plastic food container with about 10 cm of old aquarium water. Gentle aeration will improve the hatch rate. The eggs hatch after one to two weeks and the small larvae will require a constant supply of sieved *Daphnia*, newly hatched brine

42.   Axolotl, *Ambystoma mexicanum*, a species of salamander which never grows up!

shrimps or chopped *Tubifex*. Uneaten food should be siphoned off a few hours after feeding and the water replenished with fresh. As they grow the larvae will accept progressively larger prey. Cannibalism is quite common, especially once the larvae begin to increase in size, as some will grow faster than others. For optimum results, therefore, they should be continuously sorted into groups of similar-sized individuals. Another common problem is the loss of limbs, gills or pieces of tail: this may take place during feeding times or if the larvae go without food for more than a day. Missing pieces of anatomy will regenerate, however, so long as the damage is not severe and the injuries do not become infected with fungus or bacteria. The best way of guarding against infection is to keep the water clean and well aerated – treatment with methylene blue or malachite green, both obtainable from aquarium suppliers and given at the prescribed dose rate for fish – is effective in controlling fungus on eggs and larvae. If the larvae are fed well and good water quality is maintained, they may reach sexual maturity within one year.

Tiger salamander, *Ambystoma tigrinum*

The tiger salamander is a North American species with a wide range. It grows to about 30 cm, has a flattened head and small but prominent eyes. The mouth is fixed in a permanent grin. Several distinct populations are recognized, some more attractive than others, but the basic coloration is brown or olive-brown with irregular blotches of light brown, grey, yellow or cream. All subspecies make good subjects for the indoor or outdoor vivarium, however, and are more responsive than many other species of amphibians, following the movements of their keeper by patrolling along the front of their cage in the hope of food. They can be kept as described on page 106. If they are kept outside, it will be necessary to guard against excessively cold conditions, a minimum of 5°C being maintained.

Captive breeding seems not to have taken place often but should be attempted in spring when the adults will require access to water. The eggs are attached to aquatic vegetation and the larvae should be reared under the same conditions as those described on page 93.

Spotted salamander, *Ambystoma maculatum*

The spotted salamander bears a close superficial resemblance to certain forms of the European fire salamander. It is dark grey to black and well marked with numerous rounded blotches of yellow or orange.

The care of the adults is as described on page 106; breeding as on page 93.

Marbled salamander, *Ambystoma opacum*

The marbled salamander, though only about half the size of those mentioned above, is the most beautiful. It is dark grey to black in colour with about a dozen pale silver-grey bands across its body and tail. The bands often meet on the flanks and are brighter and more noticeable in the males.

This species is apparently fond of drier situations than others in the genus and its breeding habits are rather different. The adults mate and spawn in the autumn. They utilize the bottom of dried-up pools, laying their eggs in damp leaf-litter and other forest debris. The females stay

43. The attractive barred subspecies of the North American tiger salamander, *Ambystoma tigrinum mavortium*.

with their eggs until fresh rain fills the pools again. Development then continues through the winter, often beneath ice, and is completed the following summer.

There appear to have been no serious attempts to breed this species in captivity. It would seem to be a fairly straightforward affair if the animals were kept in a suitable outside enclosure with a pool (or a grassy depression) where the water level could be controlled. Indoor breeding may prove rather more difficult. Despite the complications this would be a worthwhile species to breed as its natural habitat, throughout the eastern parts of North America, is slowly disappearing.

SIMILAR SPECIES

The genus *Ambystoma* includes a number of other species which are similar in appearance to those listed. Although many of them are smaller, there are several that are attractive and interesting, and it is probably safe to assume that their requirements will be broadly similar.

CHAPTER 13

Plethodontidae: Lungless Salamanders

Although the Plethodontidae is the largest family of salamanders, only a relatively few species are at all popular as vivarium subjects. This is because they are, in general, small, secretive and rather drab in coloration. Several specialize in living in caves and underground bodies of water.

Care of these species varies according to their origin. The majority are North American and these require conditions similar to those described for the *Ambystoma* species (Chapter 12): that is, damp vivaria with subdued lighting, not too warm and with a good covering of leaf-litter and a selection of hiding places. Alternatively, many species fare very well if kept in outside enclosures with a simulated woodland-type habitat. Many tropical South American species, such as those belonging to the genus *Bolitoglossa*, are small and arboreal, living among epiphytic plants. These would require a more elaborate set-up, with appropriate plants and a temperature in the region of 25°C. There are also aquatic species, including the many North American species of *Desmognathus* (dusky salamanders), but these are not generally available. All the species are active and can move surprisingly quickly, easily capturing insect prey such as crickets. Alternative food includes earthworms, spiders and other small invertebrates.

The breeding habits of these species vary. The eggs of the most common species – the woodland salamanders, genus *Plethodon* – are laid in small clumps beneath logs or buried in damp moss. They have no aquatic larvae but hatch directly into small versions of the adults. Captive breeding is more likely to take place in an outside enclosure, where the onset of spring will stimulate the animals to come into breeding condition naturally.

44.   Northern red salamander, *Pseudotriton ruber*: beautiful but delicate.

Slimy salamander, *Plethodon glutinosus*

The slimy salamander, is a common species growing to about 15 cm in length. Its body is slender and its tail long. It is dark grey to black in colour, liberally sprinkled with smaller, lighter-coloured flecks. The common name originates from the animal's habit of secreting a glue-like substance from the skin whenever it is handled (although several other *Plethodon* species also do this).

Care is as described on page 112. This species is hardy and lives well in an outside enclosure throughout the year. Captive breeding is unknown.

113

45. Spring salamander, *Gyrinophilus porphryticus*, an unusual species which requires cool, wet conditions, sometimes difficult to provide.

SIMILAR SPECIES

Most other *Plethodon* species are smaller than the slimy salamander but would require similar living conditions. Two species which are sometimes offered are the red-backed salamander, *P. cinereus*, and the Appalachian woodland salamander, *P. jordani* (which may, in fact, consist of more than one closely related species).

Northern red salamander, *Pseudotriton ruber*

The northern red is one of the most beautiful salamanders. Adults are uniformly coloured reddish orange and have the upper surfaces peppered with black spots. As they become older the background colour darkens to dull purple. They grow to about 15 cm but are usually rather smaller than this and have slender, slimy bodies. They live in specialized habitats which can be difficult to duplicate in captivity. In nature they are found only among moss and other low vegetation where there is a constant seepage of cool, clear water, often from a nearby spring. A system of circulating chilled water would almost certainly be necessary if they were to be maintained for any length of time. Almost nothing is known regarding their breeding habits.

CHAPTER 14

Sirenidae: Sirens

The sirens form a small family of three North American amphibians which are distinct from all other salamanders. They are slender, eel-like creatures with tiny fore-limbs, no hind-limbs and external gills. They are totally aquatic or mud-dwelling and live in ditches, streams and lakes, often where these are heavily vegetated or have a thick layer of organic debris on the bottom. Two species, the greater siren, *Siren lacertina*, and the lesser siren, *S. intermedia*, are large, growing to 75 cm and 65 cm in length respectively. They feed on crayfish, molluscs and other large aquatic invertebrates. The dwarf siren, *Pseudobranchus striatus*, however, grows to only about 15 cm in length. It is often found among the roots of floating water hyacinth plants which are common in the waters where it lives. Being smaller, it feeds mainly on small aquatic invertebrates, including worms and insect larvae. Almost nothing is known about the reproductive habits of any of these species.

Sirens are rarely seen in captivity, but are easily accommodated. Young lesser sirens, for instance, will thrive in a simple aquarium set-up with no substrate but a thick growth of Java moss in which they will spend almost all of their time. The floating fern *Salvinia* can be grown on the surface to diffuse the light further. Dwarf sirens would also be happy with this arrangement but for them the water hyacinth would make a more appropriate surface plant. Earthworms are readily eaten, probably by all three species, although adults of the two larger ones may require more substantial prey items (or large numbers of worms!). Since nothing is known of their life-cycle it is difficult to suggest guide-lines for breeding them, but a suitable regime would probably involve temperature manipulations – cool winters, possibly followed by increased day length in the spring – and fluctuations in the water level. Here is an area where amateurs could make important contributions towards our knowledge of these mysterious amphibians.

PART III
Frogs and Toads

CHAPTER 15

Discoglossidae: Painted Frogs and Related Species

Although the Discoglossidae is a small family of only eleven species, it contains several that are well suited to vivarium culture. These are attractive and interesting frogs which adapt well to captivity and are often a far better choice than many of the more exotic-looking frogs and toads which, sadly, live only a short while in confinement.

Painted frog, *Discoglossus pictus*

The painted frog is a small semi-aquatic species from parts of southern Europe. It is variable in colour but is typically grey or tan with darker spots and blotches, each of which may be surrounded by a rim of a paler hue. It breeds very readily in a shallow outside pond or in a cold-frame type of enclosure, but seems not to do so well in the close confinement of an indoor vivarium. The eggs are laid throughout the spring and summer, deposited singly or in small clumps. The tadpoles are easily reared on fish flake and so on, and the young froglets will eat the smallest size of crickets, aphids and small worms such as *Tubifex*. Although the painted frog is quite a hardy species, it will not survive severe winters. For this reason it should be overwintered in a frost-free building or brought indoors to be kept warm and active throughout the winter months.

SIMILAR SPECIES

Two other species are recognized, from Sardinia and Corsica (*Discoglossus sardus*) and from Israel (*D. nigriventer*). These are not generally available, the latter being on the verge of extinction.

Midwife toad, *Alytes obstetricans*

The midwife toad comes from western Europe. It is a small grey or brown animal with an interesting life-cycle. The male's call consists of

119

a pleasant single note, often likened to the faint ringing of a bell. Mating takes place on land and, as the female lays her short string of 15 to 30 eggs, the male wraps them around his hind-legs as he fertilizes them. A male may mate successfully several times and can carry up to three strings of eggs. He visits a pool or a puddle every so often in order to dunk the eggs, so preventing them from drying out. After four to six weeks the eggs begin to hatch and at this point the male takes them to a quiet body of water and releases the tadpoles. Subsequent development is normal.

In captivity, the midwife toad does extremely well if kept in an outside enclosure or coldframe. There should be a small pool for breeding purposes and a jumble of rocks or logs on the land. The soil should be sandy and friable to enable the animals to burrow down under the rocks or logs. Shrubby or creeping vegetation will help to maintain areas of damp soil during dry weather. If the enclosure is kept

46.   Midwife toad, *Alytes obstetricans*.

open, a certain amount of natural food will be attracted and this can be supplemented with small insects, worms and slugs. Although the toads are secretive, they will emerge to forage in the evening and sometimes during the day if the weather is damp and overcast. Under this regime midwife toads will hibernate and breed naturally. It may be necessary to cover the enclosure with glass during very severe weather and, in the summer, some protection from marauding cats may be necessary. Otherwise the colony will more or less look after itself. A number of small 'free-range' colonies have been established in gardens in various parts of the British Isles over the years and several of these have thrived and even spread to surrounding gardens.

By contrast, attempts to breed midwife toads in the controlled environment of an indoor vivarium nearly always fail. The main requirements, if they are to be kept indoors, are to give them as large a cage as possible, to keep them cool and to spray them frequently in order to maintain a moist (but not wet) environment.

SIMILAR SPECIES

There are two other species in the genus but they are hardly ever seen in captivity. *Alytes cisternasii* is found in Portugal and *A. muletensis* comes from Mallorca in the Balearic Islands. The latter species is found in a remote mountainous part of the island and was described only as recently as 1977. It has been bred successfully by several zoos and the resultant young have been released back into habitat.

Yellow-bellied toad, *Bombina variegata*

Toads of the genus *Bombina* are known collectively as yellow-bellied or fire-bellied toads. They are marked with bright yellow, orange or red undersides, which they display by arching their backs should they feel threatened. This warns potential predators that they secrete poisonous substances (which are harmless unless ingested). Captive specimens very rarely display.

The yellow-bellied toad, *B. variegata*, grows to just over 4 cm, is pale greenish-grey on top and, as its name suggests, yellow beneath, with varying amounts of black. There are several subspecies, distinguishable most easily by the extent and shape of the black markings on the underside.

In nature these frogs inhabit small temporary pools of water, having been found breeding in the puddles formed in cart ruts and even hoof prints, for instance. This makes them ideally suited to a small captive set-up. They require a semi-aquatic vivarium with a hiding place on

121

the land area and some aquatic plants in the water. The toads will spend most of their time 'hanging' in the water, with just their eyes and nostrils above the surface, patiently waiting for something edible to blunder by. They feed on all the usual insect fare as well as aquatic and terrestrial worms.

Breeding activity is stimulated in the spring by bright, sunny weather and, in indoor cages, can often be triggered by moving the cage to a sunny spot. At the right time of year a complete water change is often enough to encourage breeding. The male grips the female in front of her hind-limbs (inguinal amplexus), in contrast to most other frogs and toads in which the male grips the female just behind the fore-legs (axillary amplexus). If the female is not ready to lay her eggs (or if another male is grabbed by mistake), there will be a short release call. Otherwise the pair will stay in amplexus for several hours, often spawning overnight. The eggs are usually scattered singly or in small clusters, sometimes loosely attached to aquatic vegetation. They should be removed from the vivarium to be reared separately in an

47.   Yellow-bellied toad, *Bombina variegata*: recommended for small outside pools and enclosures.

aquarium with about 15 cm of water. Their care and development follows the usual pattern. The newly metamorphosed toads are very tiny and can eat only insects such as aphids or newly hatched crickets. They are most conveniently reared, however, on *Tubifex* worms, placed in a millimetre or two of water in a shallow dish and cut into several pieces with a pair of sharp, pointed scissors.

In temperate climates, where the temperature rarely if ever exceeds 30°C, it may be more satisfactory to house this species outside. If a series of small pools is constructed in a rockery, for instance, it may be possible to keep them without close confinement as they will rarely stray more than a few centimetres from the edge of the water. If, for some reason, it is preferred to keep them in an enclosure, this should be situated in an open part of the garden where it will receive as much sun as possible. One or more small ponds should be available to them, and these should be shallow and less than 1 sq m in area. It is important to ensure that the pond is also exposed to sunshine so that the water warms up quickly – this appears to be their main (or only) breeding requirement. Under these circumstances the toads will breed several times throughout the spring and summer, provided they are fed adequately, and the tadpoles can be removed for rearing in aquaria or they can be introduced into another small pond. Overwintering the adults in an outdoor enclosure can lead to losses unless some arrangement is made to protect them from extremes of temperature. They will survive temperatures of about 5°C but no lower, and it is usually advisable to bring them indoors for the winter if there is any danger that this requirement cannot be met.

Fire-bellied toad, *Bombina bombina*

The fire-bellied toad comes from northern Europe and, like its yellow-bellied relative, is greenish-grey on top; however, its underside is bright orange-red with black markings. Although it too adapts well to captivity, indoors or out, the fire-bellied toad hardly ever breeds, although there appears to be no obvious reason why this should be so. Care is as described for the yellow-bellied toad.

Oriental fire-bellied toad, *Bombina orientalis*

Of the Asian species, the oriental fire-bellied toad, *Bombina orientalis*, is one of the most commonly available amphibians through the pet trade. Provided it is in good condition when obtained (often it is not), it will thrive and even breed under fairly simple conditions. This toad is

123

almost unbelievably colourful. The back is bright green with black blotches, the underside brilliant scarlet and black. Males are slightly more rough to the touch than females and their fore-limbs are thicker.

This species is slightly larger than the two members of the genus already described, growing to about 5 cm. Its cage should be correspondingly larger: a floor area of about 0.5 sq m would be sufficient for a group of five or six individuals. The cage should be divided into land and water areas during the breeding season. This arrangement can be maintained all year round or the toads can be moved to a totally terrestrial set-up for the winter. The breeding season begins in April and mating is often stimulated by a partial water change and sunlight. Up to 150 eggs are laid singly or in small clumps and these should be removed for rearing in a separate aquarium. The tadpoles begin to metamorphose four to eight weeks later, depending on temperature and the amount of food given, and the young toads are reared in the same way as the other *Bombina* species. With good feeding they will reach breeding size within one year.

Oriental fire-bellied toads reared in captivity do not develop the intense red coloration of wild stock. This is due to a lack of the pigment-producing chemicals in their diet and can be corrected

48. Oriental fire-bellied toad, *Bombina orientalis*, the most attractive species in the genus and fairly easily kept and bred in captivity.

naturally or artificially. If the young frogs are fed on large numbers of small crustaceans such as *Daphnia* and *Gammarus*, the red coloration will develop naturally. Alternatively, an artificial colouring agent can be added to their food and this will have a similar effect. Colour foods sold for feeding to tropical birds and fish all contain carotene, the chemical precursor required, and if small amounts of this are sprinkled on the *Tubifex*, the red coloration will develop quite quickly. This 'problem' also effects other *Bombina* species, although to a lesser extent, and the solution in all cases is the same.

Giant fire-bellied toad, *Bombina maxima*

The giant fire-bellied toad is a second species from the Far East which has been available in the past. It is less frequently seen than the oriental fire-bellied toad, however, and has not been bred with as much success. It is slightly larger than *B. orientalis*, growing to about 6 cm as opposed to 5 cm, and is wartier. It has a greenish-grey back and an orange underside. This species appears to prefer deeper water than the others in the genus and will stay active at lower temperatures, down to 10°C at least. Although the adults may breed in the spring, in

49. Amplexus in fire-bellied toads and other discoglossid frogs is inguinal: that is, the male grasps the female immediately in front of the hind-limbs.

response to a longer day length and warmer conditions, and the tadpoles are quite easily raised, growth of the young toads is slow. They appear to dislike *Tubifex* and must be fed on insects such as fruit flies and young crickets, of which an abundant supply is necessary. Again, the addition of carotene to their food will enhance their coloration.

This species' tolerance of low temperatures may qualify it for outdoor culture. It is so rarely seen, however, that experiments of this kind would be rather risky.

SIMILAR SPECIES
There are reports of two other species of *Bombina* in China, but these have probably never been imported into Europe or North America.

CHAPTER 16

Pipidae:
Clawed Frogs and
Related Species

The family Pipidae comprises twenty-seven species from South America and Africa. Members of three of the four genera are fairly widely available from time to time, and several species have been bred in captivity.

All species are totally aquatic. They have large, webbed hind-feet and a more or less flattened body. They feed on almost any living thing small enough to fit into their wide mouths and several species will also accept dead fish and strips of meat.

African clawed frogs, *Xenopus* species

The most commonly seen species of clawed frog are *Xenopus laevis*, *X. muelleri* and *X. tropicalis*, all from Africa. Although they differ in size, their appearance is similar. They are grey in colour with small, round eyes situated towards the top of the head. A row of sense organs runs down each flank, looking rather like a row of stitches. There is an albino strain of *X. laevis* in captivity, often known as the 'golden clawed frog'.

All *Xenopus* species are easy to care for and require the minimum by way of accommodation. They should be kept in aquaria with about 10-20 cm of water, heated to about 20°C. The small species, that is, *X. tropicalis* – can be given a substrate of gravel and some rockwork, but in general these frogs are so clumsy that they will quickly wreck an elaborate set-up. They will eat small fish, earthworms and aquatic insects. Some will take small strips of meat or liver offered on forceps, though this diet is unsatisfactory in the long term and will also foul the water quickly. Breeding is usually achieved only after the toads have been given a hormone injection; however, it is possible to breed them naturally. This is usually accomplished by allowing the water to evaporate gradually until only a few centimetres remain, then replacing it with

50.   A small species of clawed frog, *Xenopus tropicalis*.

51.   The albino form of the African clawed frog, *Xenopus laevis*, sometimes known as the 'golden clawed frog'.

cold water to simulate rain. The method is not always successful and may have to be repeated several times before breeding occurs. The tadpoles are rather unusual in that they are filter feeders. They hang in mid-water, tail up, and gulp mouthfuls of water. This is forced through specialized organs which sieve out particles of food. In captivity they are most easily raised on liquid fish-fry food, a few drops of which should be added to the water several times each day. Only when the tadpoles have cleared the water should more food be added. When the froglets have metamorphosed they switch to a carnivorous diet, which is most conveniently supplied in the form of *Tubifex* worms. They are easily raised.

Dwarf clawed frogs, *Hymenochirus* species

Hymenochirus is also an African genus, possibly consisting of four species but reduced to two, *H. curtipes* and *H. boettgeri*, by some authorities. Both of these are sometimes available, often arriving in the company of tropical fish. They are not easily told apart: *H. curtipes* is said to have shorter legs and small eyes whereas *H. boettgeri* has longer legs and is also characterized by spiny tubercles on the sides and thighs. These differences are hard to perceive in such small, dark-coloured frogs but, as their care and breeding is identical, it is probably not too important to know which species is concerned. Both grow to about 3.5 cm and are brown above, sometimes speckled with darker spots, and dirty white to cream below. Males develop small, pale glands immediately behind their front legs but, in my experience, these are not easily seen. Again, males have a larger tympanum (eardrum) than females, but this is not easily assessed either. A better means of telling the sexes apart is afforded by the body shape, females being noticeably rounder than males. Unfortunately, if they are not well fed prior to purchase, all individuals may appear thin, masking any obvious difference. Since the frogs are often available cheaply from tropical fish dealers, the best plan is to buy a group of six to ten individuals and house them together, allowing them to pair at will once they are conditioned.

They require an aquarium with 10-20 cm of water heated to 20-25°C. It is important to cover the tank well or they may climb out. Because of their small size it is easy to arrange the set-up attractively, with a gravel or sand substrate, some rocks or bogwood and some plants. Java moss, *Vesicularia dubyana*, is a good choice, along with a floating plant such as *Salvinia*, which will diffuse the light. The adults require a diet of *Daphnia*, bloodworms and *Tubifex* worms. They will

129

52. Dwarf clawed frog, *Hymenochirus boettgeri.*

also eat small fishes, given half a chance. Breeding can take place at any time of the year if the animals are well fed, although a small rise in temperature may be needed to stimulate them. Males call beneath the surface with a strange clicking trill. Amplexus is inguinal and, after some preliminary 'push-ups' by the male, the pair rise to the surface of the water, then turn over on to their backs while the female deposits several eggs at the surface and the male fertilizes them. This sequence is repeated several times until all the eggs, numbering up to 1000, have been laid.

The eggs should be removed from the parents' aquarium to prevent them from being eaten. The small tadpoles are carnivorous and will need ample supplies of microscopic live food at first. This can be supplied most easily by adding a few drops of pond water to their aquarium or, preferably, by rearing them in an established aquarium in which a good micro-fauna will already be present. As the tadpoles grow they can be given small *Daphnia* (poured through a fine sieve) and newly hatched brine shrimp. Eventually they will begin to meta-morphose, by which time they will be large enough to eat the same food as the adults.

Surinam toad, *Pipa pipa*

Sometimes known as the pipa toad, the Surinam toad originates from northern South America where it inhabits murky ponds and swamps. This bizarre animal grows to about 20 cm in length and is greatly flattened. The front legs are short and each digit ends in a small, star-shaped organ which appears to be sensitive to touch. The hind-legs are large and powerful and the hind-feet are huge and flipper-like. It has very small eyes, which are in any case probably of little use in its natural habitat. The body is dark grey above and pale grey or off-white below, and there may be some degree of mottling. Females can be distinguished from males by a ring-shaped swelling at the cloaca. This is apparent only when the animals are in breeding condition, however. The species has a remarkable life-cycle, very similar to that of Carvalho's toad which is described overleaf.

53. Surinam toad, *Pipa pipa*. A female carrying eggs embedded in the specialized pad of skin on her back.

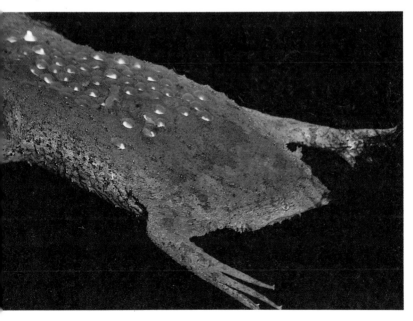

It requires a good depth of water in a covered aquarium. A temperature of about 20-25°C is required at all times. Lighting should be subdued and there should be plenty of cover in the form of bogwood and plants such as Java moss. It will feed on small fish (such as goldfish), earthworms and other fairly large aquatic invertebrates. Breeding is as described for *Pipa carvalhoi* below.

Carvalho's toad, *Pipa carvalhoi*

Carvalho's toad is very similar in appearance to the Surinam toad, only much smaller and not quite so flat. It also differs in its life-cycle (see below).

Its general biology and care in captivity are similar to that of *Pipa pipa*, although it will also eat pieces of meat. Breeding is fairly easy in *P. carvalhoi* but problematic in *P. pipa*. In both cases the males make a ticking call from beneath the water. Amplexus is inguinal and, once the female has been stimulated to lay, she will swim to the surface repeatedly and the pair will turn over. On each visit to the surface several eggs will be laid, the male will fertilize them and then manoeuvre them on to the female's back with the help of his large hind-feet. A full complement of eggs is about 100 in *P. pipa*, 200 in *P. carvalhoi*. Once egg laying is completed, the pair separate with the female now holding all the eggs on her back. Over the next twenty-four hours a specialized pad of skin will swell around the eggs, embedding them in a thick, spongy layer, each egg forming a separate chamber where its development will take place.

The two species differ in their subsequent development. The young *P. carvalhoi* are released when they are tadpoles and they subsequently develop in the same way as the tadpoles of *Xenopus* – that is, they are filter feeders. They can be reared on liquid fish-fry food or, since they are quite large, they will take small pieces of fish flake from the surface. They will require separate accommodation from the adults to prevent their being eaten. The larval *Pipa pipa*, on the other hand, are retained in their chambers until they are fully developed. This takes twelve to twenty weeks. They then escape from the female's back, usually at the same time as she sheds her skin. Their first food is small aquatic invertebrates such as *Daphnia* and *Tubifex*. Once the young tadpoles or toads have been released, the skin on the back of the females returns to normal.

CHAPTER 17

Pelobatidae: Spadefoot Toads

The family Pelobatidae has a wide distribution, with members in North America, Europe and South-east Asia. The North American and European species belong to the genera *Scaphiopus*, *Spea* and *Pelobates*, whereas the Asian species are divided into several genera of which the horned frog, *Megophrys nasuta*, is the only well-known species.

North American spadefoot toads, *Scaphiopus* and *Spea*

The North American spadefoot toads all come from more or less arid environments. They escape desiccation by burrowing down into the sand or soil until they reach a level where some moisture is retained. Here they further protect themselves by making a cocoon consisting of several layers of shed skin. When heavy rains fall they burrow to the surface and breed immediately, so that their tadpoles have a reasonable chance of metamorphosing before the pools and puddles dry out.

Although there are six species altogether, the most attractive is probably Couch's spadefoot toad, *Scaphiopus couchii*, which is yellow with brown reticulations. Like the other members of the family it has large, prominent eyes and a sharp, horny projection on its 'heel' which helps it to dig backwards into the ground (and which gives it its common name).

This species requires a semi-arid vivarium with a substrate of sandy soil or fine grit and a temperature of 20-25°C in the summer. It may be allowed to become considerably cooler in the winter. It will spend the daylight hours beneath the surface, emerging at night to eat small invertebrates, such as crickets and waxworms. It seems that breeding in captivity has not been achieved, but in all probability this could be stimulated by allowing the vivarium to dry out slightly, then spraying the surface with water until part of it became flooded.

54. Couch's spadefoot toad, *Scaphiopus couchii*, one of the more attractive of the spadefoot clan.

European spadefoot toad, *Pelobates fuscus*

Pelobates fuscus, the most common of the European spadefoot toads, is sometimes known as the garlic toad because of the smell it gives off when handled. Originating from Central Europe and growing to about 8 cm, it prefers to live in sandy soil into which it burrows during the day. It cannot, however, tolerate the extreme dry conditions of its North American relatives, and in captivity the substrate should be kept slightly moist at all times. It will eat small insects and other invertebrates. Breeding in a vivarium has probably not been achieved, but this species would be a good choice for an outdoor enclosure in a warm, sheltered location. Given the right conditions and an ample supply of food, it would probably breed successfully.

Asiatic horned toad, *Megophrys nasuta*

The Asiatic horned toad, a large, tropical pelobatid, is totally different from the above species in both appearance and habits. It is unmistakable

55.   Asian horned toad, *Megophrys nasuta*, which makes a superb exhibit provided the correct conditions can be maintained.

with its sharply pointed snout and pointed projections over each of its inky-black eyes. The back is brown or reddish-brown and shaped and coloured like a dead leaf. When crouched on the rainforest floor this frog is almost impossible to see, even if its exact location is known. For this reason most of the imported animals are males, which have been located by their calls. Females are very rarely seen in captivity but are easily identified as a result of their much larger size: they grow to about 15 cm, whereas the males are only about half this length.

Horned frogs usually do well in captivity provided they have been well cared for during collection and importation – unfortunately they often arrive in very poor shape and are doomed from the start. They require a terrestrial rainforest-type environment with a good layer of leaves and leaf-litter. If leaves from tropical plants can be included, so much the better. A temperature of 25°C is required constantly. They also need hiding places, such as 'caves' made from pieces of curved bark. They usually feed well on large insects such as crickets, half-grown locusts and, especially, cockroaches.

Because of the problem in obtaining females, breeding is rarely attempted. They require a large cage with an area of shallow water. Pieces of bark and bogwood should be arranged over the water so that the female can attach her eggs to their undersurfaces, just above the water level. The tadpoles slide down into the water when they hatch. *Megophrys* larvae have highly specialized, funnel-shaped mouths which take several days to develop. Then they will feed only from the surface of the water and can be reared on floating fish flakes.

SIMILAR SPECIES

There are several other species of *Megophrys* from South-east Asia, including one, *M. longipes*, which lays its eggs on land, where they develop without water. Related genera also occur in the same part of the world but appear in the pet trade only rarely. Little is known of their requirements, although a set-up as described for the horned toad would probably be a good starting point.

CHAPTER 18

Bufonidae: True Toads

The Bufonidae is a large family of almost 350 species. The majority are placed in the genus *Bufo*, which also has the widest distribution, but several other genera are recognized. Bufonids are typically stout, warty toads with a dry skin and brown, grey or greenish coloration. They often live in semi-arid environments, at least for part of the year, and some are especially desert-adapted. Some species, however, are from tropical rainforests and other wet places and these may differ from the general description in being smooth-skinned and, in some cases, brightly coloured. Only one species, *Pseudobufo subasper*, from Malaysia, is completely aquatic.

Very many bufonid species occur in the pet trade from time to time but their care and breeding has not been well documented except in a few instances. Only a relatively small number of species can be dealt with here in any detail; however, the information should be useful in assisting with the creation of satisfactory conditions for a number of similar species.

1: EUROPEAN SPECIES

European common toad, *Bufo bufo*

The familiar *Bufo bufo* is the archetypal toad: stout in build, dry to the touch and warty. It grows to 10 cm in most parts of its range, but examples from southern Europe sometimes reach 15 cm. The coloration varies, usually being some shade of grey, greyish-brown or reddish-brown, but the most prominent feature is the eye, which is a brilliant copper colour. Males of this species tend to be smaller than females and develop black nuptial pads on the insides of their first three digits.

56. European common toad, *Bufo bufo*, usually maintained in a semi-wild state in an outdoor enclosure or greenhouse.

In northern Europe, and in other parts of the world with a similar climate, this toad, and others like it, are ideal subjects for an outdoor enclosure. They require a well-drained site with plenty of hiding places and a small pond for breeding. Their food consists of all the usual insect prey as well as worms and slugs. Many enthusiasts prefer to let them live more or less at liberty in a suitable part of the garden or in a greenhouse, for example, where they will be beneficial in keeping down pests.

Breeding takes place in the spring and amplexus is inguinal. The female lays her eggs in a long string containing several thousand eggs. These usually hatch without problems and the tadpoles are easily reared. With adequate feeding they will metamorphose between two and three months later. If a few are moved indoors to an aquarium, these will grow more quickly. The young toadlets are small and require aphids, fruit flies and so on at first, but it is often better to release them in a suitable spot outdoors and allow them to forage for food naturally.

Natterjack toad, *Bufo calamita*

The natterjack is smaller than the common toad, reaching a maximum length of about 8 cm. It is prettily marked with a yellow vertebral stripe down its back and a ground colour of olive-green. The warts on the flanks may have a pinkish tinge.

The natterjack toad requires similar conditions to the common toad, but the soil in its cage or enclosure should be sandy. Permanently waterlogged conditions should be avoided. Although it will thrive indoors, breeding is possible only in outdoor enclosures with warm, shallow pools. Under these conditions it should breed every spring. The mating season begins later than that of the common toad as this species requires warmer conditions. The tadpoles take two to three months to metamorphose and require very small sized food to begin with. The natterjack toad is protected in most parts of Europe.

Green toad, *Bufo viridis*

The green toad replaces the natterjack, to which it is closely related, in parts of eastern Europe. Although most specimens lack the yellow vertebral stripe, its coloration is most attractive, being putty-coloured with large green blotches and reticulations.

The care and breeding of this species are identical to that of the natterjack toad.

57.   Green toad, *Bufo viridis*.

2: NORTH AMERICAN SPECIES

American toad, *Bufo americanus*

The American toad grows to about 10 cm and is common over much of eastern North America. Unlike the European common toad, males of this species have a vocal sac and call loudly. Its general care is as for *Bufo bufo* and it would probably breed under similar conditions, but there appear to have been no attempts to breed this species.

SIMILAR SPECIES

The same remarks apply to a number of similar species from the same region, such as the southern toad, *Bufo terrestris*; Fowler's toad, *Bufo fowleri*; and the Gulf Coast toad, *Bufo valliceps*.

Red-spotted toad, *Bufo punctatus*

The red-spotted toad is a desert species, found in the south-western corner of North America, often in the company of spadefoot toads, whose habitat it shares. It is quite small, growing to a maximum of about 7.5 cm, and is attractively marked with numerous small red spots on a grey background. This species climbs well and is less plump than many other *Bufo* species.

In captivity it will do very well in a cage with a substrate of moist sand or sandy soil and a jumble of rocks to provide hiding places. It requires a summer temperature of 20-25°C. Insects and other invertebrates are eaten, but it seems to prefer the more active species, including mealworm beetles. Breeding has apparently not been attempted; however, the conditions suggested for the American spadefoot toads (see page 133) should also apply to this species.

SIMILAR SPECIES

The American green toad, *Bufo debilis*, comes from similar areas and would probably have similar requirements in captivity. It is an attractive species, mainly yellowish-green with irregular black markings, but is seldom offered, however. The western toad, *Bufo boreas*, is a larger species, growing to 10 cm or more. It is olive or greenish above with a thin cream line running down its back. Although it also lives in desert regions, it appears to be restricted to damper micro-habitats, often along man-made irrigation and drainage ditches, for instance. In captivity it may be treated in the same way as the European natterjack and green toads. Numerous other species of toad are found in the

58.   Southern toad, *Bufo terrestris*, from south-eastern North America.

59.   Red-spotted toad, *Bufo punctatus*, a desert species which is undemanding in captivity.

drier, western parts of North America, but these rarely appear on the market. It may be assumed that their care in captivity is similar to the species mentioned, although detailed information is sadly lacking.

TROPICAL AND SUBTROPICAL SPECIES

There are so many species of toad throughout the tropics that it is difficult to select a manageable number to describe here. By choosing one species from each of three continents, South America, Africa and Asia, I hope to give some indication of the general conditions under which a wider range of toads can be maintained.

Cane toad, *Bufo marinus*

Bufo marinus, a large and common species, is also known as the marine toad and the giant toad. It is a native of South America, where it has a wide range, being especially common around villages. In addition it has been introduced to Australia, to control sugar-cane beetles (which it failed to do and has since become a pest). The cane toad grows to 20 cm in length and is brown in colour. Some individuals are marked with blotches of light and dark brown, but most are plain. It has prominent parotid glands, from which a noxious substance is secreted if the toad is annoyed. Additional poison glands are found on the thighs.

This species is generally undemanding in captivity. It needs a temperature of about 25°C, a substrate of moist, sandy soil or leaf-litter and somewhere to hide – a large clay flower pot usually does the job admirably. It will accept a wide range of prey, the only requirement being that this will fit into its mouth. Large examples will therefore eat mice, young rats and other frogs and toads in addition to the usual insect fare. *Bufo marinus* is clearly therefore not a species for a community cage! Although it may lay up to 30,000 eggs in the wild, no records of captive breeding are known.

SIMILAR SPECIES
Other large South American toads include Blomberg's toad, *Bufo blombergi*, which may be even larger than the cane toad, and the rococo toad, *Bufo paracnemis*, which is about the same size. Blomberg's toad has been bred in zoological gardens on more than one occasion but it requires an enormous vivarium with elaborate environmental control. Both species are also protected internationally.

Moroccan toad, *Bufo mauretanica*

Bufo mauretanica is a North African toad, grey in colour with dark, sometimes maroon blotches on its back. It grows to about 12 cm.

In captivity this species has similar requirements to the European natterjack toad (see page 139), to which it is closely related. Furthermore, it will breed in outdoor enclosures as long as these are sited in such a way as to provide optimum warmth: that is, they are south-facing and covered with glass during cold spells of weather.

SIMILAR SPECIES
Very few other African toads come on to the market, but the square-marked toad, *Bufo regularis*, has been available from time to time. This is the most common African species (although it is divided into a number of different species by some authorities). It has a wide range and its markings are correspondingly variable. It is easy to keep as it tolerates a wide range of temperatures and will eat most insects and other small invertebrates. It is unlikely to be fully hardy, however, and is best kept in an indoor cage.

Black-spined toad, *Bufo melanostictus*

A common Asian species, the black-spined toad is similar in size to the European common toad but is attractively marked with jet-black tubercles on a pale buff background. It is usually found around human settlements.

60.   Black-spined toad, *Bufo melanostictus*, a common species which appears to do quite well in captivity.

In captivity it requires a temperature of about 25°C and the usual diet of insects, worms and slugs. There is no information on breeding this species in captivity.

SIMILAR SPECIES
Bufo asper is the largest Asian bufonid, sometimes exceeding 20 cm in length. An inhabitant of primary rainforests, it is sometimes found a metre or so off the ground in stumps and hollow trees. It often has a pink or reddish tinge to its otherwise grey coloration. In captivity it fares reasonably well, but requires a large cage with warm, humid conditions.

61.   Young *Bufo asper*, an agile South-east Asian species which requires tropical conditions.

3: OTHER BUFONIDS

Harlequin frogs, *Atelopus* species

The harlequin frogs are South and Central American species which often bear little superficial resemblance to typical bufonids. There are over forty species in all, several new ones having been discovered recently. A few live at very high altitudes in the Andes and these are plump with short legs and frequently dark in coloration. There are considerable difficulties in keeping these specialized toads in captivity. The lowland species have slender bodies and long, spindly legs. Many of them are brightly coloured, paralleling the poison-dart frogs from the same geographical region.

Very few of these species ever find their way into the pet trade. Furthermore, there has been little success in keeping and breeding them in captivity. They would appear to require well-planted cages with high humidity and good ventilation. An area of running water will help to create the correct conditions. Temperatures should not be too high, 20-25° being adequate. They have hearty appetites and require a constant supply of small insect food such as fruit flies, newly hatched crickets and small worms such as *Enchytaeus* (whiteworms).

CHAPTER 19

Rhinodermatidae:
Mouth-brooding Frogs

The family Rhinodermatidae contains only two species, both in the genus *Rhinoderma*. The only well-known one is Darwin's frog, *R. darwinii*. It occurs in the beech forests of southern Chile and southern Argentian and is remarkable for its breeding habits.

Darwin's frog grows to about 3 cm in length and has a sharply pointed snout. It may be bright green, brown or yellow-brown on the back, but its ventral surface is always black with white blotches. The eggs are laid on the ground in clutches of thirty to forty. The male stays nearby until the tadpoles begin to wriggle about inside the jelly and then picks them up in his mouth. They remain inside his vocal pouch for about three weeks and there is evidence to suggest that he produces a nutritious secretion on which they feed while they are developing and growing. When they are fully developed froglets, he spits them out.

Darwin's frogs have been imported into Europe and North America in small numbers at various times. They require cool conditions, no more than 20°C, and a substrate of dead leaves or bark chippings which should be kept just moist. They feed on small active insects. Imported males may be holding broods of tadpoles which they later release. These are very small and frail and rarely survive, possibly as a result of stress incurred through capture and shipping. The adults seem to do quite well in captivity, but there have, unfortunately, been no successful attempts to breed them on a regular basis.

CHAPTER 20

Leptodactylidae: Leptodactylid Frogs

The Leptodactylidae, a large family of over 700 species of frogs and toads, is restricted to North, Central and South America. Many of its members are small, nondescript species, but others are spectacular and fascinating.

Horned frogs, *Ceratophrys* species

The horned frogs, of which there are six or seven species, are among the most unmistakable and weird species in the pet trade. They appear to have been morphologically designed, and psychologically programmed, for one purpose only: to eat as much as possible. At first glance they seem to consist of two parts, a mouth and a stomach! They do have legs, of course, but these are small and almost insignificant, serving only to move them from one meal to the next. Little wonder, then, that horned frogs and their close relatives have captured the imagination not only of dedicated amphibian enthusiasts but also of the general pet-buying public.

Thanks largely to the efforts of herpetoculturalists in North America, these frogs are now freely available commercially, in the form both of species and of hybrids. The care and breeding of the most popular forms is similar.

Argentinian (or Bell's) horned frog, *Ceratophrys ornata*

The Argentinian horned frog may grow to a length of almost 15 cm, although the male is noticeably smaller than the female, rarely exceeding 10 cm. These statistics give no impression of size, however, because the frogs can easily be as wide as they are long. Furthermore, their heads, and therefore their mouths, are almost as wide as the body. The coloration of this species is rather variable. The most colourful forms

62. Argentinian horned frog, *Ceratophrys ornata*, a popular and simply-kept pet.

are mainly green with a good scattering of red markings. Others are darker, with extensive black markings and only small areas of green.

All the South American horned frogs are secretive by nature and spend a large part of their life beneath the ground. Activity is stimulated by rain or high humidity. Their diet consists of just about anything which will fit into their enormous mouths, including smaller frogs (even of the same species), fish and small rodents. Insects are the main diet of juveniles. Prey is taken by a sudden lunge forward and may be helped into the nether regions of the mouth by the front feet. This species can sometimes be aggressive towards larger animals, including humans, and can give a painful bite. Captives usually settle down quite quickly, however, and can be handled with ease.

Care of this species is very simple. It requires a constant temperature of around 25-28°C but occasional drops in temperature, for instance at night, will not normally be harmful. Accommodation consists, in its simplest forms, of a plastic box or an aquarium containing shallow water and one or two rocks arranged in such a way as to allow the frog to climb out. The depth of the water will depend on the size of the frog: as a rough guide it should cover about half of the frog. A layer of pea gravel can be spread over the bottom of the aquarium and this will give the frog a better grip, although cleaning will be more time-consuming. Food, consisting of large insects or worms, should be placed on the emergent rocks, although insects and so on will also be

63. Argentinian horned frog – a closer look.

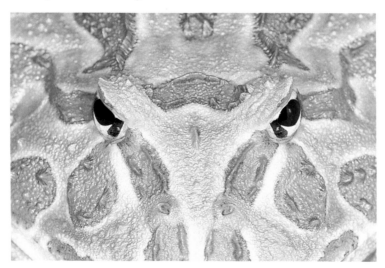

taken from the surface of water. Dead mice of an appropriate size can be offered by hand or forceps. It is recommended that horned frogs are housed singly except when breeding in order to avoid the possibility of cannibalism. Food can be offered twice to week to young specimens, but this may be reduced to once every week for adults.

Sex determination is not possible in juvenile horned frogs, although, as has already been noted, adult males are considerably smaller than females and they also develop darker throats and conspicuous nuptial pads, especially when in breeding condition.

Breeding in captivity is usually achieved after a course of hormone injections. An overview of this technique is given in Chapter 7. It can, however, be induced naturally by cooling the adults off for a period of two to three months (to a minimum of 20°C) and then warming them up. As they are warmed up they should be 'rained upon' with cool water for several hours each evening. This is best achieved by housing the frogs in a 'rain chamber', with an overflow built into their aquarium and a pump sending fresh water from a reservoir to a sprinkler system installed around the rim of the tank (see Chapter 7). Furthermore, females respond most positively if a recording of male calls is played to them frequently over a period of several days.

The eggs, numbering over 1000, are wrapped around aquatic plants or an artificial substitute, which should be made available to them. They hatch after only twenty-four hours. The tadpoles are predatory and require a constant and plentiful supply of small aquatic inverte-brates such as *Artemia*, *Daphnia*, whiteworms and bloodworms. If sufficient food is available, their cannibalistic tendencies will be kept under control, although a small proportion, mostly runts, will 'dis-appear'. Most breeders favour the housing of small groups: this reduces the risk of large-scale losses resulting from predation or disease.

At a temperature of 30°C the tadpoles grow rapidly and the first ones may begin to metamorphose after only three weeks. The young froglets are especially cannibalistic and it is now essential to house them singly. Since they require only a small amount of space, this can be achieved by keeping each one in a small plastic food container or in sections of plastic pipe standing in a tray of shallow water. With constant feeding, sexual maturity is reached in about eighteen months.

Chacoan horned frog, *Ceratophrys cranwelli*

The Chacoan horned frog is similar to its Argentinian relative but has a slightly larger, more bony head and the horns over its eyes are more pronounced. Juveniles are not as brightly coloured as those of *C. ornata*, but later develop red, orange and yellow markings. The care and breeding of this species is identical to that of *C. ornata* and it has also been hybridized with that species. The resultant offspring share the characteristics and markings of both parent species but are more vigorous and may grow even larger than either of them.

Surinam horned frog, *Ceratophrys cornuta*

The Surinam horned frog has the most obvious horns in the genus. It is smaller than either of the above species, is less colourful and its snout is more pointed. It has proved rather difficult to maintain and breed and grows more slowly. It appears to prefer a diet of frogs and/ or fish. This species has also been hybridized with *C. ornata* and *C. cranwelli*, producing attractive offspring which fare rather better in captivity than the pure species.

SIMILAR SPECIES

Four more species are recognized in the genus *Ceratophrys*. All are from South America and all have the general body plan of the species described: short, fat and with a wide mouth. None of these other species is freely available at present, but there is hope that commercial breeders will turn their attention to some of them over the next few years, adding to the variety within this interesting group of amphibians.

Budgett's frog, *Lepidobatrachus laevis*

Budgett's frog is closely related to the horned frogs and is placed in the same subfamily, Ceratophrynae. With a flattened body and short limbs, it lacks the horns of the Ceratophrys species. It has small, round, bulbous eyes and a smooth, grey skin. Females grow to about 12 cm in length; males are noticeably smaller, to about 10 cm. In the wild, Budgett's frog spends the greater part of each year aestivating beneath the ground in order to avoid the dry winter conditions which prevail in its habitat.

Young, captive-bred juveniles are very occasionally available but are expensive because the costs involved in rearing them are high.

The ideal requirements for breeding are still uncertain. The care of Budgett's frog is similar to that of the Argentinian horned frog, but the water can be deeper, just covering the animal's back. This species will eat insects and small rodents, yet can also be fed on fish such as guppies and, later, goldfish. Individual housing is recommended, to avoid competition for food, and cannibalism.

Breeding follows a period of aestivation, during which time the adults are removed from their aquatic quarters and housed in a container of moist soil into which they will usually burrow. A water bowl should be included in the container, however, in case they are not ready to aestivate. The soil should be kept slightly moist throughout this period by occasional light spraying. Up to the time of writing, all successful spawnings have been induced by hormone injections but, with experimentation, it should be possible to persuade the frogs to reproduce naturally, probably by using a 'rain chamber' as described on page 75.

The tadpoles of this species are predatory and cannibalistic and should be housed singly or in small groups of similar-sized individuals. There is some evidence to suggest that the tadpoles need to ingest particles of grit or soil to aid in digestion, and so a thin layer should be placed on the bottom of each rearing container. The first food of the tadpoles is *Artemia* or other small invertebrates. Their appetites are large and they quickly graduate to small fish (or other tadpoles). When they are ready to metamorphose, the water level should be reduced until it is approximately one and a half times the height of the froglets.

64. 'Dwarf' Budgett's frog, *Lepidobatrachus llanensis*.

The diet of small fish can be continued or they can be switched to insects such as crickets, dusted with good-quality vitamin/mineral supplement.

SIMILAR SPECIES
There are two other species in the genus *Lepidobatrachus*. Of these, *L. llanensis* is also bred commercially and may be available from time to time. It is marginally smaller than Budgett's frog and has warty skin and patches of yellow at the base of the fore-limbs. It is equally accommodating in captivity under identical conditions.

Eleutherodactylus species

The frogs belonging to the genus *Eleutherodactylus* have no common name. Although most are small and rather drab in appearance, they have an interesting life-cycle and can be kept quite easily in captivity. They are recommended for housing in colonies in large, well-planted vivaria. Over 400 species have been described so far, from Central and South America and the Caribbean Islands. *E. planirostris* has been introduced into Florida from Cuba. Of those which are sometimes kept in captivity, the whistling frog, *E. johnstonei*, is probably the best known. Details on its care and breeding in captivity will serve as a guide to the care of the other members of the genus.

65. 'Dwarf' Budgett's frog – a closer look.

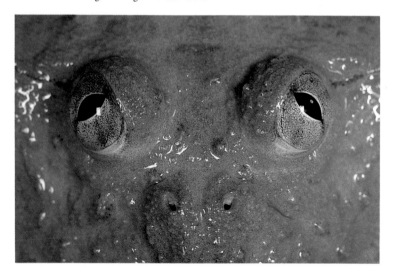

This species comes from the West Indies and, like its congeners, is tiny: females reach a maximum size of about 3 cm and males are slightly smaller. Females are plain brown in colour, whereas males may have slightly darker lines or chevron-shaped markings on their backs. Whistling frogs are easily accommodated, the only problem being obtaining an adequate supply of insects small enough for them to eat. A simple set-up could consist of an aquarium with a 5-10 cm layer of leaf-litter on the bottom. A few large leaves or pieces of bark will serve as hiding places and egg-laying sites. One or two pot plants placed towards the back of the cage would enhance its appearance as well as providing additional surfaces for the frogs to climb and a humidity gradient. Since the frogs prefer subdued light, ferns and/or mosses would be most appropriate. Certain bromeliad species would also thrive under these conditions. There is no need to provide a water bowl.

A temperature of 20-25°C should be maintained throughout the year, an underfloor heat-pad being the most convenient means of arranging this. The cage should be sprayed occasionally to maintain a humid environment, although adequate ventilation should not be neglected. Fruit flies, *Drosophila*, are a convenient size for the frogs, but other invertebrates of similar size should be given whenever available, sieved sweepings being especially recommended. Newly hatched crickets will also be accepted, but great care must be taken not to introduce too many or the escapees will survive and grow in the vivarium, eventually damaging the plants and, more importantly, attacking any eggs that may be laid.

In such a set-up, breeding will commence without any special stimulus. The males make a persistent but not unpleasant, whistling call, usually from an exposed calling site which will be used regularly. Amplexus takes place on land and is rarely seen. The relatively large eggs are laid in clumps of ten to twenty-five and are hidden in a damp place beneath a piece of bark or log. There is no free-living tadpole stage, the eggs hatching directly into small froglets measuring a mere 5-6 mm in length. Development takes about twelve days, from laying to hatching. The newly hatched froglets are too small to eat the same food as the adults and the very smallest grade of sweepings must be made available to them. Perhaps the most convenient technique is to place a fresh handful of leaf-litter in the cage every few days and allow the froglets to find the small, almost invisible micro-fauna which is thus introduced. Aphids and springtails are also excellent food. As a rule there is no need to separate the eggs or the young from the breeding stock and the cage can be maintained as a self-sustaining colony.

66. *Eleutherodactylus* species from South America. The 400-odd species in this genus are mostly plain in coloration, but they have an interesting life-cycle and are very suitable for keeping in planted vivaria.

SIMILAR SPECIES

Theoretically, almost any of the 400-odd other species of *Eleutherodactylus* could be kept in similar conditions to those described above. In practice, however, they are rarely available, because they have little obvious appeal when compared to the more colourful tropical species which form the bulk of the pet trade. One species, as yet unidentified, turns up quite regularly (in the UK) in shipments of bananas from the West Indies. Unfortunately, it appears only singly and there have been no opportunities to attempt breeding.

In one species, *Eleutherodactylus jasperi*, the eggs are fertilized internally and development takes place in the oviduct (that is, it is ovoviviparous). Another, *E. coqui*, sometimes known as the golden coqui, also practises internal fertilization but lays eggs.

OTHER LEPTODACTYLIDS

Leaving aside the ceratophrynes and the members of the genus *Eleutherodactylus*, there are several other genera belonging to the family Leptodactylidae. Those in the genus *Leptodactylus* are superficially similar to the familiar *Rana* species but lay their eggs in foam nests. This breeding behaviour is also seen in several other genera, notably *Physalaemus* and *Pleurodema*. These and other species are rarely, if ever, imported by the pet trade as there is hardly any interest in them and they have little value commercially.

CHAPTER 21

Dendrobatidae: Poison-dart Frogs

The common name of the family Dendrobatidae is derived from the fact that South American Indians use the strong toxins, produced in the skin of these frogs, to tip their blowpipe darts. It is now established that the use of this practice is restricted to about three species only, however, and that some species produce very low levels of toxins. In captivity the toxins appear gradually to lose their potency and, with one possible exception, *Phyllobates terribilis*, there is no reason why these frogs cannot be safely reared in the home provided that sensible precautions, mainly washing the hands after handling the animals, are carried out.

The poison-dart frogs (sometimes known as the poison-arrow frogs) are a group with a very special place in the amphibians hobby: they have achieved what is almost a cult state amongst herpetoculturalists, especially in Holland and Germany where some enthusiasts keep their frogs in huge, room-sized vivaria, thickly planted with vines, brom-eliads and orchids. The reasons for their popularity are not difficult to understand. Dendrobatids combine unbelievably bright coloration with bold, diurnal activity patterns and they adapt readily to captivity provided a few simple rules are adhered to. Furthermore, they are the perfect subjects for attractive, planted vivaria which can be an asset to any home if properly constructed and maintained.

On the down side, many of them live in very restricted areas, often just a few hectares or less, and for this reason they all enjoy some measure of international protection. As most species breed readily in captivity, however, there seems no reason why the availability of the more common species should not continue.

The family Dendrobatidae numbers over 100 species altogether and is restricted in distribution to Central and South America (there is also an introduced population of one species on Hawaii). Several species have been described recently from remote and isolated parts of Amazonia and from the Andean foothills, and there is no doubt that many more await discovery. They are partially arboreal (*Dendrobates* means 'tree-dweller' in Latin), although some species are more often found on or near ground level. On the other hand, some of the more recently described species live exclusively in the crowns of tall rainforest trees – and are therefore only seen when the trees are felled.

The nomenclature of this small family is in a state of chaos, several revisions having been published in the last fifteen years or so. Although this is not the place for a taxonomic discussion, some effort is made here to clarify the situation so that breeders' lists and recent literature can be followed.

The first major revision, by Silverstone in 1975 and 1976, divided the species into three genera: *Dendrobates*, containing sixteen species; *Phyllobates* with twenty species; and *Colostethus* with just over forty species. (*Colostethus* species are not brightly coloured and are not usually included in the collective common name of 'poison-dart frogs'.) In 1978 Myers, Daly and Malkin revised the relationships of the genera *Phyllobates* and *Dendrobates*, leaving just five species in *Phyllobates*, the other fifteen being added to those already in *Dendrobates*. The genus *Colostethus* remained unchanged.

More recent research has seen the descriptions of several more species, hitherto unknown, and yet another revision to include some of these new species as well as to re-organize the previously known species. At the time of writing, twenty-three species are included in a new genus, *Epipedobates*; eight in a second new genus, *Minyobates*; while twenty-six remain in *Dendrobates* and five in *Phyllobates*. In addition, a totally new species of dendrobatid has been described recently and placed in another new genus, *Aromobates*. The genus *Colostethus* has not received as much attention over the years, although a trickle of new species has been added to it.

In summary, the Dendrobatidae, as currently recognized, includes the following genera:

Aromobates	1 species
Colostethus	50 species approximately
Dendrobates	26 species
Epipedobates	23 species
Minyobates	8 species
Phyllobates	5 species

Of these 100-plus species, a large proportion of the *Dendrobates* and *Phyllobates* species are kept and bred in captivity by specialists, many of whom keep no other amphibians, whereas a relatively small number are in general circulation. Only the latter is considered here.

GENERAL CARE AND BREEDING OF DENDROBATIDS

Poison-dart frogs should be kept in spacious, well-planted vivaria, preferably with running water. Their cages should be heated to a constant temperature of about 25°C, using an underfloor heat-pad, and they should be well lit, for the benefit of both plants and frogs. Most enthusiasts prefer to use epiphytic plants, especially miniature orchids and bromeliads, attached to pieces of driftwood. Irregular chunks of tree fern root are also used extensively as these encourage the growth of tropical mosses, many of which will begin to grow spontaneously once the material is damp and the temperature raised. It is not strictly necessary to include an area of open water in the cage unless the colony is to be allowed to breed without external manipulation: that is, unless the eggs are to be left where the frogs lay them.

Instructions for constructing suitable systems can be found on pages 49-52.

The need for good ventilation cannot be overstressed. Although some species seem to be able to tolerate a stagnant, soggy atmosphere, they will all thrive best in a cage with a good rate of air change. If large areas of the lid contain mesh, ventilation will be good but evaporation will take place rapidly. This will necessitate frequent spraying (several times each day if practicable) or the installation of a system of running water. If the latter arrangement is used, it will be necessary to keep a check on the water level or the pump may run dry. Small electric fans, such as those used to keep computers cool, have been used with success to keep the air circulating and there is great scope for improvisation and experimentation in this area.

Lighting is best provided by fluorescent tubes, using as many as possible in order to encourage healthy plant growth. Provided the level of lighting is adequate it is not essential to use horticultural-type tubes, those of a warm-white colour being satisfactory. It may be necessary, however, to use a natural-spectrum light source for rearing the tadpoles (see page 80). Some cage designs make use of the heat generated by the light starter units to raise the temperature of the cage during the day, when the lights are on.

Feeding dendrobatids can become a time-consuming business. Because they require vast quantities of small insects, most enthusiasts with large collections find that culturing their own food is the only viable proposition. Fruit flies, *Drosophila*, are the most useful species, although adults of the larger dendrobatids will also take hatchling crickets and graded sweepings. Unless fruit flies are used more or less exclusively, however, it is difficult to avoid introducing plant pests unless great care is taken to ensure that all food is eaten as soon as it is offered. The frogs will quickly learn to come out of their hiding places and feed at the front of their cage immediately food is placed there: this provides a useful opportunity to check on the health and breeding condition of the animals as they resent disturbance at other times. All food should be well dusted with a vitamin and mineral supplement before use. For animals which are actively breeding and for young, growing animals, feeding several times each day is advantageous if it can be arranged. A small colony of poison-dart frogs can easily consume several thousand fruit flies over the course of a week or so.

Newly metamorphosed young are extremely small in some species: several are not large enough to take even fruit flies and an alternative food must be made available. Aphids are suitable but there is rarely a sufficient and reliable supply, and great care must be taken to ensure that they have not been sprayed with an insecticide before they are gathered. Springtails are widely used by breeders of the smaller species. These are available only through other dendrobatid enthusiasts and must be cultured at home. The only way of finding such a source at the time of writing is through one of the specialist societies listed at the back of this book. As several methods of culture are used, instructions should be sought from the supplier.

Poison-dart frogs will begin to breed without any special stimulus. If the temperature and humidity are suitable, and the animals are in good condition and well fed, the females will soon swell with eggs and the males will begin calling. In the wild the eggs are laid out of water on a smooth, clean and moist surface, such as a leaf. The number varies from species to species. Under the natural course of events, one or other of the parents watch over the eggs until they begin to hatch. They then encourage the tadpoles to climb on to their backs, where they attach themselves lightly. The laden parent finds a small body of water in which to release the tadpoles and they continue to develop without further attention. There are some variations, however. A small group of species, of which *Dendrobates pumilio*, is the best-known example, take each larvae in turn to a separate place, often the small volume of water which accumulates in the vase of a bromeliad plant, where it lives, grows and develops in isolation. Furthermore, the females of these species visit each site every day or so and lay one or more infertile eggs in the water to provide food for the larva. This type of life-history is among the most remarkable in the animal kingdom but is, unfortunately, difficult to replicate in the confines of a vivarium.

In captivity suitable places for egg laying must be provided. These

159

consist of secluded areas with a smooth, clean surface. A common method is to invert half a coconut shell, with an entrance hole, over a glass or plastic petri-dish or a watch-glass. Although the frogs will lay directly on the glass or plastic surface, it can be advantageous to place a layer of kitchen paper towelling or, better still, a small piece of capillary matting (as used in horticulture) in the dish. This makes removal and subsequent hatching of the eggs more convenient. Other breeders use a variety of similar structures, or the frogs may be allowed to find a suitable leaf for themselves. One advantage of providing laying sites is that they can be inspected regularly, allowing any recently laid eggs to be discovered and removed. Obviously there must be at least one laying/calling site for each male, and it is good idea to provide one or two extra places in case some are unsuitable.

It is generally considered advantageous to remove the eggs and rear them and the tadpoles separately. The eggs, together with the substrate on which they have been laid, should be placed inside another container which is then covered to prevent excessive evaporation. If the eggs are laid on a leaf or a piece of capillary matting or other material, this should be placed in a shallow dish and flooded with a millimetre or so of warm water: this prevents them from drying out. Some breeders prefer to keep warm water flowing over the eggs by means of a gentle system of circulation, but this has not proved to be essential. The eggs take about two to three weeks to hatch, and when hatching begins the water level should be raised to the top of the egg mass. As the tadpoles wriggle away from the egg mass they can be scooped up in a teaspoon and transferred to rearing containers.

It may be necessary, depending on the species, to rear each tadpole individually in a small glass or plastic container: this avoids the possibility of cannibalism and enables individual attention to be given. Laboratory beakers, plastic food containers and so on are suitable. The water should be maintained at about 25°C: this can be done by keeping individual containers in a warm room, or by standing them together in a large container which holds several centimetres of water, heated by an aquarium heater with a thermostat (that is, in a waterbath).

It should be noted that a few species can be more simply reared as they will live and develop together in a small aquarium or, if appropriate, in an aquatic area built in to the adults' cage.

Tadpoles are most easily fed on fish flake, but additional meals of brine shrimp, whiteworms and so on are also beneficial. Tadpoles of the *Dendrobates pumilio* group should be fed on egg yolk, but it must be said that rearing these species has not so far been very successful. A vitamin and mineral supplement can be given in the form of a small pinch added to the water in each container once every week. All uneaten food should be removed a few hours after feeding and replaced with aged water at the same temperature. Water from an established aquarium tank is ideal but tap water which has been aerated and left to stand for at least twenty-four hours is usually satisfactory. The most efficient way to remove the dirty water from the containers is to use a narrow polythene tube, such as a length of airline tubing, fitted with a narrow glass spout. Damage to the tadpoles must be avoided as they are very prone to fungal infections.

If large numbers of tadpoles are being reared, the business of changing the water in each container becomes rather laborious. Various designs have been used to get around this problem, usually based on a number of small perforated glass or plastic cells through which water can be circulated.

The tadpoles take about ten weeks to reach metamorphosis. Once the legs have emerged, each tadpole should be moved to a small, shallow dish which is then placed inside a planted vivarium. Several of these shallow dishes may be put in the same vivarium. In order to ensure an immediate food supply for the young of the smallest species, the vivarium must be seeded with springtails. These tiny invertebrates will thrive in the warm, moist environment, but they must be obtained well before they are needed so that their population can build up in the culture (see page 159). The froglets will be large enough to take fruit flies in about one month. They should be reared in small groups of five to ten individuals to avoid unnecessary competition and will be sexually mature within about one year. As stocks in captivity are limited, and to avoid the dangers of inbreeding, it is a good idea to try to exchange some of the offspring with other breeders before they reach maturity.

SPECIES DESCRIPTIONS

Only brief descriptions are given here. Notes on care and breeding are supplementary to the rather lengthy information given above.

Green poison-dart frog, *Dendrobates auratus*

The green poison-dart frog was among the first bred in captivity and is still a favourite. Although several colour forms are recognized, the most widely seen is black with irregular bands and blotches of beautiful metallic green. They grow to about 5 cm. Care is as described above. This species breeds readily, usually laying six to eight eggs.

161

67. The green poison-dart frog, *Dendrobates auratus*, is one of the better-known and more popular species.

Blue poison-dart frog, *Dendrobates azureus*

This fabulous species reaches about 4.5 cm in length and its coloration is predominantly bright blue, with rounded spots of black on its back. The limbs are a deeper shade of blue. This is a very rare species with a limited distribution, but there are several captive colonies. Care and breeding are as described above.

Red-and-black poison-dart frog, *Dendrobates histrionicus*

The red-and-black poison-dart frog occurs in a bewildering variety of colours and patterns. A common form is brown with a multitude of yellow and orange spots on the head and body. Others are black and yellow or black and red. The boldly banded, black-and-bright-red form is now known as *D. lehmanni*, but the two species are closely related and their care is similar. These species have proved to be among the most difficult to breed. The tadpoles feed on egg yolk, but even when eggs are laid they rarely hatch. *Dendrobates histrionicus* should be avoided by beginners and is only included here because it is one of the more frequently illustrated and listed species.

162

68.   The blue poison-dart frog, *Dendrobates azureus*, must rate as one of the most beautiful amphibians. It was discovered only in 1969 and is bred on a limited scale by dedicated enthusiasts.

69.   The yellow-and-black poison-dart frog, *Dendrobates leucomelas*, is one of the easier species to keep, but has a rather nervous disposition.

Yellow-and-black poison-dart frog, *Dendrobates leucomelas*

Dendrobates leucomelas is more stocky and robust than most, achieving a length of about 4 cm. It is black with deep yellow bands across the top of the head, around the mid-body and over the hind-limbs. The yellow bands are broken with irregular blotches of black. Juveniles have clear yellow bands. Care and breeding are as described above but this species can take larger prey such as small waxworms. Up to ten eggs are laid and as the tadpoles are not inclined towards cannibalism they can be reared communally if this is more convenient. A recommended species.

Strawberry poison-dart frog, *Dendrobates pumilio*

Highly variable in coloration but usually bright red, the strawberry poison-dart frog is a small species rarely exceeding 2.5 cm. It has a specialized life-history, outlined above, and is very difficult to maintain and breed in captivity.

Dyeing poison-dart frog, *Dendrobates tinctorius*

The dyeing (NB, not dying!) poison-dart frog is among the largest in the group, sometimes growing to 6 cm in length. Once again, this is a variable species. Typically it has a blue underside marbled with black, while the back and flanks are black with yellow dorso-lateral stripes. It requires a larger vivarium than most other species and will tackle larger prey, including crickets. Otherwise the care and breeding are as described above. Up to twenty eggs are laid in a clutch.

Epipedobates tricolor

This species is similar to another, *Epipedobates anthonyi* and there is some confusion over the correct naming of captive stock: they may be *E. tricolor*, *E. anthonyi* or there may be some of each. For the time being, however, I will assume that they are *E. tricolor* as this is the name they are usually found under. The care and breeding of both species is likely to be identical in any case. This is one of the easiest species to keep and breed and is highly recommended, even for beginners. It grows to about 2.5 cm, and despite one of the scientific names, *tricolor*, the markings consists of just two colours, three longitudinal cream stripes on a brick-red background. The limbs are also marked with cream.

70. Dyeing poison-dart frog, *Dendrobates tinctorius*, one of the most striking
species and one which usually does well in captivity.

This accommodating and engaging species, though not as spectacularly marked as some of the others, has much to recommend it. It is very active, moving around the vivarium and calling frequently, and will eat a wide variety of insect food, including crickets and waxworm larvae. Under ideal conditions it will breed continuously throughout the year. In addition it breeds so successfully in captivity that it is readily available at a reasonable price.

The female lays up to forty eggs at a time. These are transported to water by the male and it is not strictly necessary to remove them from the vivarium provided that a small body of water is available. Most breeders divide the cage in such a way that about one third of the floor area is water; this can also act as a reservoir if water is circulated through the cage. The larvae will live together without problems and should be fed on fish flake. They reach metamorphosis in six to eight weeks. By keeping the frogs in a self-perpetuating colony, all sizes and ages will be present at the same time. This makes an interesting display and interaction between individuals can be observed easily. They should not be allowed to become overcrowded, however, or rival males will fight and may devour one another's eggs. Serious breeders intending to obtain the maximum number of offspring favour removal of the eggs and rearing the tadpoles in a separate aquarium.

71.   *Epipedobates tricolor.* Easy to keep and breed, this is perhaps the most suitable species for beginners to try.

72. *Dendrobates truncatus*, another small species which breeds well in captivity.

73. *Phyllobates bicolor*. Two frogs interacting: although courtship may be involved, it is more likely that these are two males engaging in territorial combat.

Phyllobates bicolor/terribilis

Phyllobates bicolor grows to 4 cm in length and is uniform yellow or orange with black feet and a black underside. Care and breeding are as described above. The female lays up to thirty eggs and the larvae can be reared communally if required. This species is often confused with *Phyllobates terribilis*, a more recently described species with extremely toxic skin. The latter is slightly larger, however, and usually lacks the black markings on the limbs and underside, being plain yellow or orange in colour. Its care and breeding are also as given above.

Lovely poison-dart frog, *Phyllobates lugubris*

A small species, growing to 2.5 cm in length, the lovely poison-dart frog has a glossy black back with two narrow orange dorso-lateral stripes. The limbs are marbled with metallic bronze and the underside is pale blue-grey. Care and breeding are as described above; it is a relatively easy species to keep. Females lay up to twenty eggs and the tadpoles can be reared communally.

74. *Phyllobates vittatus*, a colourful and easy-to-keep species.

75.   A *Colostethus* species from Ecuador. The frogs in the genus are not as colourful as the better-known poison-dart frogs, but are usually easy to keep and breed.

Striped poison-dart frog, *Phyllobates vittatus*

Phyllobates vittatus is similar to *P. lugubris* but slightly larger. The dorso-lateral stripes are wider and the limbs are more colourful, often greenish. Care and breeding are as described above. Up to twenty eggs are laid and some breeders leave these in the vivarium as described for *Epipedabates tricolor.* This is probably the easiest of the *Phyllobates* species to breed and is recommended.

Colostethus species

Because of their comparatively sombre coloration, the *Colostethus* species have never earned as much attention from dendrobatid enthusiasts as those discussed above. They are interesting frogs, however, with a similar life-history to the other members of their family. *Colostethus trinitatus* has been bred in captivity on a number of occasions. It grows to about 3.5 cm in length and is predominantly brown in colour, with dark, mottled flanks. The throat of males is brown, that of mature females yellow. Females, as well as males, are territorial in this species, but a large vivarium will provide plenty of space for several individuals.

CHAPTER 22

Hylidae: Tree Frogs

The tree frog family consists of about 630 species with a collective range covering most of the warmer regions of the world. Although most are adapted to an arboreal way of life, with expanded toe-pads and moderate size, others are more terrestrial and there are even a few burrowing species in the family. A number of distinct groups of species are of interest to vivarium keepers because of their attractive coloration or interesting life-cycle, or both. These groups are dealt with separately in order to avoid repetition.

Note that frogs of several other families are often known as 'tree frogs' in the pet trade. If the species concerned is not listed here, it may be covered under one of the following: reed frogs (Hyperoliidae), Chapter 24; or Asian and African tree frogs (Rhacophoridae), Chapter 25.

1: PHYLLOMEDUSINES

Members of the subfamily Phyllomedusinae are found only in Central and South America. They number about forty species in all, mainly brightly coloured, large, slow-moving tree frogs which are highly arboreal. They share the same reproductive habit of attaching their eggs to the leaves of palms and other vegetation overhanging water.

Red-eyed tree frog, *Agalychnis callidryas*

The spectacular red-eyed tree frog grows to about 7 cm in length, although the males are invariably smaller than the females. Its dorsal surface is bright grass-green while its flanks are blue with cream bars. And as if this were not flamboyant enough, its feet are orange and its large eyes are brilliant red.

76.   Red-eyed tree frog, *Agalychnis callidryas*, a species which epitomizes exotic tropical tree frogs.

Red-eyed tree frogs are occasionally offered for sale and have been successfully bred on a number of occasions. They require large vivaria with a minimum of one cubic metre for a group of three or four. High humidity and a temperature of at least 23°C are required. The cage should be furnished with branches or, preferably, living plants, which should be fairly robust. The frogs will eat insects such as moths and crickets, but care should be taken to give only small numbers of the latter in order to avoid stressing the frogs.

They are strictly nocturnal and spend the days crouched on the underside of a leaf or in a corner of the cage. At night they will begin to move around and feed. It often takes several weeks before newly

171

acquired animals settle into their accommodation and during this time they should be disturbed as little as possible.

Breeding may take place spontaneously or it can be encouraged by manipulating the humidity. In either case an area of water is required and this is best arranged by partitioning the floor of the cage. The depth of the water is probably not too important but, for ease of management, there should be a reasonable volume: a minimum of, say, 10 litres. If the cage is kept fairly dry for a while, by arranging plenty of ventilation and spraying them only occasionally, the adults will become less active. Care must be taken not to allow them to become dehydrated, however. After a dry period the cage can be sprayed several times each day or 'rain' can be produced automatically by means of sprinkler and a timer, as described in Chapter 7. Alternatively, if the cage contains a system for circulating water, this can be turned off for several weeks and then turned on again in order to increase the humidity. Whichever system is used, an increase in humidity will often stimulate the males to call. Provided the females have been well fed and are in good health, spawning should take place within a week of the first calls being made.

The eggs are laid above the water level, ideally on a large leaf overhanging the water area. If a leaf is not available, the females may lay on the sides of the vivarium, but this is not such a satisfactory arrangement. The eggs hatch five days after they are laid and the tadpoles wriggle themselves to the tip of the leaf, then drop off into the water. Just before this occurs, the leaf can be removed from the cage and suspended over a freshly set-up aquarium to receive the tadpoles. Alternatively, the tadpoles can simply be removed from the parents' cage with a dip net and placed in the separate rearing aquarium. The latter arrangement allows subsequent females to use the same leaf should they so wish.

The tadpoles are quite easily reared on fish flake and so on, but extra calcium should be incorporated into their diet to prevent deformities. For the same reason it may be beneficial to use a natural-spectrum light or a blacklight (see page 68) in the cage where the newly metamorphosed froglets are housed. Subsequent rearing is best done by housing the young frogs in small groups – for instance, in clear plastic food containers – and keeping them on a substrate of moist kitchen paper towelling or foam for the first few weeks.

SIMILAR SPECIES

A further seven species are placed in the genus *Agalychnis*. Although it is assumed that their requirements would be similar to those described for *A. callidryas*, they appear not to have been bred in captivity.

77. All phyllomedusine tree frogs lay their eggs in leaf nests overhanging water. This is *Phyllomedusa trinitatus*, one of the more unusual species.

78. *Phyllomedusa tomopterna*, a large and colourful South American species.

Phyllomedusa species

The thirty-odd species in the genus *Phyllomedusa* are all bright green in colour. Although they have large eyes, they are not red. With one or two exceptions these species occur in South America and are rarely available through the pet trade.

Limited experience would indicate that they too require large cages with plenty of vegetation among which they can hide during the day. As stated above, all these frogs have similar reproductive habits and so a semi-aquatic arrangement such as that described would almost certainly be necessary to encourage them to breed. Unfortunately these species seem to have attracted little attention, possibly because of the difficulties in obtaining stock.

2: MARSUPIAL FROGS

There are almost sixty separate species of marsupial frog, in seven genera. Those of the genus *Gastrotheca* are the most likely to be kept in captivity and then only occasionally because of difficulties in obtaining stock. This is unfortunate, for they are attractive and interesting in addition to adapting well to captivity.

All the frogs in this subfamily are characterized by some mechanism for carrying their eggs and tadpoles on their backs. In the more primitive species, such as the five *Hemiphractus*, which are hardly ever seen in captivity, this consists merely of a small depression and the eggs are exposed. In the more advanced species, such as those belonging to the genus *Gastrotheca*, however, the female develops a pouch on her back, giving the developing eggs and larvae a high degree of protection.

Riobamba marsupial frog, *Gastrotheca riobambae*

Although marsupial frogs are often listed collectively as *Gastrotheca marsupiata*, the species which is most frequently kept is in fact *G. riobambae*. This is a variable species from Ecuador which may be plain green, green with three bronze stripes, or green with irregular bronze blotches. It grows to a length of 7 cm and is robustly built. Although it has the expanded toe-pads typical of the family, this species is more terrestrial than most, climbing only into low vegetation as a rule.

It can be kept and bred under quite simple conditions. Coming as it does from high altitudes, it is not sensitive to cold and will even live outside provided there is some protection from frost. In an indoor cage

79. Marsupial frog, *Gastrotheca riobambae*, resting in a bromeliad plant.

it can be kept on a substrate of moist leaf-litter or moss and there should be a container of water, or the cage should be partitioned. Some bark or flakes of rock will provide hiding places, although this species is quite active during the day as well as at night. It eats all manner of insects and other invertebrates of a suitable size.

In captivity, breeding takes place during the spring. The male's call is raucous, rather like that of a chicken, with a drawn-out croak punctuated by two or three 'clucks' at the end. Receptive females approach the males and amplexus takes place on land. As the eggs are laid the male fertilizes them and then assists the female by manoeuvring them into the pouch on her back. A clutch of eggs may number up to 100 or more. For the next ten weeks or so the female carries the eggs in her pouch, which becomes noticeably distended. Towards the end of this period the tadpoles, which are now well developed, can sometimes be seen wriggling beneath the female's dorsal skin. Eventually the female will sit in shallow water, open the pouch with one of her hind-toes and release the tadpoles. At the end of this process she scoops out any reluctant tadpoles, or unfertilized eggs, again using the long toes of her hind-feet.

175

80. Female *Gastrotheca riobambae* carrying eggs, which can be clearly seen swelling the pouch on her back.

The tadpoles are voracious and grow rapidly on a diet of fish flake, lettuce or aquatic plants. When they begin to develop their hind-legs, it may be advisable to suspend a natural-spectrum light over their cage as they are otherwise prone to deformed or weak limbs. Metamorphosis is complete in eight to ten weeks and rearing the froglets, which are relatively large, is straightforward. They will reach breeding size within one year.

SIMILAR SPECIES
The above species appears to be the sole marsupial frog available, and then only occasionally. Of the other *Gastrotheca* species some lay much smaller clutches of eggs but retain them for longer, not releasing their offspring until they are fully developed. This group of species is from lowland areas and would certainly require a temperature more in keeping with their origins – that is, 20-25°C.

3: HYLINE TREE FROGS

Species within the genus *Hyla* form the largest part of the family. These are typical tree frogs with a collective range covering most of the tropical and subtropical world except Australasia, where they are replaced by the closely related species belonging to *Litoria* (page 183). The *Hyla* species are small-to-medium-sized frogs with more or less expanded toe-pads and an arboreal lifestyle. Many of them are attractively marked, with greens and browns predominating. In captivity most species are fairly accommodating, but the smaller ones usually adapt best. They all require a tall vivarium furnished with branches and, if possible, planted with robust 'house plants'. Their temperature requirements will obviously vary according to the part of the world from which they originate. Certain species are suitable for keeping in heated or unheated greenhouses. All species are insectivorous and will be content with a diet of crickets and, especially, flying insects. Of the 250 or so species recognized it is possible to mention only a few of the better-known ones.

European tree frog, *Hyla arborea*

The well-known European tree frog grows to a length of about 5 cm. Its back is bright green, changing to brown under certain conditions. Bright blue specimens have been recorded in the wild on rare occasions. A bold, dark stripe running from the eye to the groin is always present.

This species is well suited to outside accommodation which must, of course, be completely enclosed. It can withstand fairly high temperatures, up to 25°C at least, provided there is adequate humidity, as well as cool nights and cold winters. It should, however, be protected from freezing and near-freezing temperatures. If kept indoors it may be housed in a large, unheated vivarium out of direct sunlight. A fluorescent tube will give a little localized extra heat which it will enjoy, often sitting on the tube for hours on end. It usually settles in quickly provided conditions are to its liking, and it is a voracious feeder on flies, moths, crickets and so on. If sweepings can be obtained they should be used as often as possible, and a mineral supplement should be dusted over the food at least once every week.

For breeding a small area of water is necessary and this should contain a good density of aquatic plants. The breeding season starts in spring and continues throughout summer. Each female will spawn more than once provided she is well fed. The male's call is somewhat raucous, to say the least, especially if several are housed together as they will call in chorus.

Females that are ready to spawn will approach their selected mate and amplexus will commence on land, then continue in the water. About 200 eggs are laid in a small clump among aquatic vegetation. These are best removed for rearing in aquaria heated to about 20°C,

81. Mediterranean tree frog, *Hyla meridionalis*, a tough and undemanding species for a greenhouse or large indoor vivarium.

and fed on algae and fish flake. They metamorphose in about two months, when they should be transferred to moist vivaria. The froglets are relatively large and can handle fruit flies, newly hatched crickets and aphids right from the start. They can be raised to maturity in one year, but two to three years is a more realistic goal.

A very closely related species is the Mediterranean tree frog, *Hyla meridionalis*. Although it has a more southerly distribution, its requirements are identical.

American green tree frog, *Hyla cinerea*

The attractive American green tree frog has become a stock-in-trade with pet shops and reptile dealers over the last ten years or so and is therefore easily and cheaply obtained. It is more slender than the European tree frog and slightly longer. It is beautifully marked, being bright grass-green above with a prominent cream line running from the angle of its jaw and along its flanks. This line is lacking in a small proportion of specimens.

82.   American green tree frog, *Hyla cinerea*. This species is one of the most frequently available hylids. It does reasonably well, but seems reluctant to breed in captivity.

179

Its accommodation should be as described for the above species but temperature must be more closely regulated and maintained at 20-25°C during summer, slightly cooler during winter. This frog also adapts well to captivity as long as it has not been stressed during shipping: often it is in poor condition when it arrives and fails to respond to even the best attention. Assuming good stock is obtained, it will thrive on the usual insect diet. Males make a loud, quacking call, sometimes known as a 'rain call' but also stimulated by extraneous noises. Unfortunately there are no records of breeding having been achieved in captivity.

American grey tree frog, *Hyla versicolor*

Despite its name, the American grey tree frog is also a beautifully marked animal, being grey or grey-green in colour with intricate darker reticulations on its back. This coloration serves to camouflage it exceptionally well when it is resting on the bark of a tree. It also has orange flash colours on the inside of its thighs, only visible when it is moving. It grows to about 5 cm and is stockily built.

Grey tree frogs do well in captivity under similar conditions to those that suit the American green tree frog. Once again there are, regrettably, no records of its having been bred in captivity.

SIMILAR SPECIES

A number of other North American tree frogs could, potentially, be available through the pet trade. Species such as the spring peeper, *Hyla crucifer*; the squirrel frog, *H. squirella*; and the barking tree frog, *H. gratiosa*; and others have all been imported from time to time. Their general care follows the same pattern as that described for *H. cinerea*. Captive breeding is not well documented.

Cuban tree frog, *Osteopilus septentrionalis*

Osteopilus septentrionalis, although a native of Cuba, has been introduced into Florida and now occurs there in enormous numbers. It can exceed 10 cm in length and, as well as enjoying large insects, is a voracious eater of smaller frogs. It must be housed separately for this reason. It is brown or greenish-brown in colour and its back is slightly rugose. It has relatively large toe-pads.

It needs a large vivarium, a temperature of about 25°C, and plenty of food. Other than this, its requirements are few and, given enough

83.   American grey tree frog, *Hyla chrysoscelis*, an expert in camouflage.

181

84. Barking tree frog, *Hyla gratiosa*, a large and well-marked species.

85. Cuban tree frog, *Osteopilus septentrionalis*, a large species which will adapt to a variety of conditions.

room, it will breed readily in captivity. It is prolific, laying up to 2000 eggs. Development is rapid and the froglets metamorphose about six to eight weeks later.

4: AUSTRALASIAN TREE FROGS

The Australasian tree frogs, originally placed in the genus *Hyla*, are now given a genus of their own, *Litoria.* Despite the lack of fresh stocks from Australia, resulting from a ban on wildlife exportation, one species has become a favourite with frog fanciers, and another, from Indonesia, is imported occasionally.

White's tree frog, *Litoria caerulea*

White's tree frog is found in north-eastern Australia and in southern New Guinea. Captive-bred and wild-caught animals are available. This species grows to a length of 10 cm and is best described as portly. It is bright apple-green above, sometimes with a scattering of irregular, pure white spots. The green coloration fades to white on the underside. The toe-pads are huge and efficient: removing a specimen from the glass sides of a vivarium, or even from the hand, can be difficult! A characteristic fold of skin runs over the eardrum, and in large (overweight?) specimens this develops disproportionately. Occasional bright blue examples have been reported in the wild but these should not be confused with the dull blue-green or blue-grey coloration of certain captive-bred stocks: for some reason, captive-raised animals rarely attain the beautiful, clear green colour of the imported specimens.

White's tree frog is well suited to captivity. In the wild it often has regular 'perches', frequently around houses, and rarely strays far in the search for food or a mate. A well-ventilated cage measuring about 1 m high × 50 cm × 50 cm would be adequate for a group of four or five adults. If breeding is the aim, the bottom of the cage should be partitioned into land and water areas; otherwise it is not strictly necessary to include water at all, so long as the substrate is kept moist and the cage is sprayed occasionally. The most practical and attractive substrates for the cage are leaf-litter or bark chippings, of which the finer grade ('orchid bark') is recommended. Because of its heavy build, this frog needs stout branches and strong plants, such as the more robust species of *Philodendron*, on which to climb. A temperature of about 25°C is required, although if the temperature drops to 20°C occasionally no harm will be done. The species is generally a good

183

86.   White's tree frog, *Litoria caerulea*, from Australia and Indonesia. This popular amphibian is long-lived in captivity and has been bred quite frequently.

feeder, enjoying large insects and other invertebrates. These should be dusted with a vitamin/mineral supplement at each feed. Some specimens will also take nestling mice. Smaller frogs are not refused either, so they should not be housed with White's tree frog.

Sexing the adults is usually quite easy, provided the animals are in good condition. Males are generally smaller than females and have a dusky throat, caused by the relaxed vocal pouch. Any animals seen calling can be confidently confirmed as males. Commercial breeding is usually achieved by the use of hormone injections, but it will also take place spontaneously if the environment is manipulated. The breeding stock must be well established and healthy. First, a period of cooling to 20°C is required. During this time they will not accept food and should be closely monitored to ensure that they do not lose weight. The cage may be allowed to dry out slightly during this period but, again, close monitoring is essential. After about two months of this regime, spawning is induced by creating artificial 'rain' several times each day, especially in the evenings. The water level in the aquatic part of the cage can be allowed to rise and the temperature should be returned to a minimum of 25°C. Calling will normally commence within a day or two and spawning should take place after about a further week or less. Each female may produce up to 3000 eggs which should be removed for separate rearing. Development and care follows the normal routine and strong lighting, especially with natural-spectrum fluorescent tubes, is recommended. Metamorphosis of the first froglets will start in about four to six weeks with adequate feeding, and they will grow rapidly so long as they are not overcrowded and sufficient food can be provided.

The newly metamorphosed young are often not bright green but a murky shade of grey. There is some evidence to suggest that the green coloration can only develop if the frogs are exposed to high levels of light. In practice, captive-bred White's tree frogs are rarely as colourful as wild-caught specimens and further research needs to done on this problem.

SIMILAR SPECIES

The white-lipped tree frog, *Litoria infrafrenata*, has been imported from Indonesia in recent years. This species grows to about the same size as White's and is also bright green. It differs, however, in being more streamlined in shape (it could hardly be less so!) and has a prominent white line around the lower lip. There is some variation according to the source of the frogs, but the brilliant green specimens often seen in illustrations are very difficult to obtain. This species does not adapt to captivity as well as White's tree frog, is nervous and may refuse to feed. Breeding has been achieved but, apparently, only by using hormone-induced spawnings.

5: THE AUSTRALIAN WATER-HOLDING FROG
Cyclorana species

This Australian species is rather an oddity. For years it had been classified along with the leptodactylid frogs, but recent research seems to indicate that it is more closely allied to the tree frog family.

A single species has been commercially bred in captivity. This is apparently *Cyclorana novaehollandiae*, a species which has been recently separated from the better-known *C. australis*. It is a chubby frog, growing to almost 10 cm in length, although males are notably smaller. The species is variable in coloration, but all the captive-bred animals so far seen have been brown with extensive bright green markings on

87. A large Australian frog, *Cyclorana novaehollandiae*, a relative newcomer to the hobby of amphibian keeping. It seems to adapt well to captivity and has a good appetite (see photograph 23).

the back, head and flanks. It is a voracious feeder, being Australia's answer to the horned frogs, *Ceratophrys*, and specializes in eating smaller frogs in the wild.

In captivity this species appears to be very undemanding. Captive-bred juveniles settle down quickly in basic accommodation consisting of a small plastic box and a moist substrate of moss, leaf-litter or kitchen paper towels. They can be housed together only if of a similar size. They feed readily on insects such as crickets, and as they grow will graduate to dead newborn mice offered by forceps. There are no details on the method of captive breeding, but it is assumed that this has been hormonally induced.

CHAPTER 23

Ranidae:
Pond Frogs and Related Species

The family Ranidae includes all the familiar 'pond frogs' or 'water frogs', genus *Rana*, in addition to a good number of lesser-known groups of species. Altogether there are over 650 of them with an almost worldwide distribution. Because of their diversity it is not possible to describe a 'typical' ranid or to deal with their care and breeding in a generalized manner. Furthermore, only a small proportion of the family is likely to be of interest to amphibian keepers, namely the *Rana* species, several of which are suitable subjects for outside vivaria or even unenclosed garden ponds; the African bullfrog, *Phyxicephalus adspersus;* and the *Mantella* species from Madagascar which compete with the poison-dart frogs for the title of the world's most colourful species. These three groups are dealt with in turn.

1: POND AND WATER FROGS, GENUS *RANA*

Although this genus includes a multitude of tropical and subtropical species, several of which sometimes occur in amphibian importations, those which are likely to be of most interest are the European and North American species which are hardy or almost hardy, and which can be kept out of doors in a suitable enclosure.

These species are medium-sized, averaging around 10-12 cm in total length. They have a pointed snout, obvious tympanum and long legs. They are predominantly brown or green in colour, are agile and lively and, for the most part, do not do well if confined to a small vivarium, where they will damage themselves by jumping at the glass sides in their efforts to escape.

Although the species vary somewhat in their temperature requirements, outside enclosures, as described in Chapter 5, or greenhouses or coldframes are the best places to keep them. The enclosure should have a sizeable pool, planted with a selection of aquatic and marginal

88. European common frog, *Rana temporaria*, spawning in an outdoor pond.

plants, if the frogs are to breed. Some species like to warm themselves in the sun and it is a good idea to place a number of large, flat rocks around the edge of the pool, or even in the pool itself, so that they can bask. A large pile of logs will provide hiding places, a hibernation site and a source of food in the form of earthworms, slugs and other invertebrates. As the populations of invertebrates will soon become depleted, they should be 'topped-up' at every opportunity. Additional insects can be attracted by growing a range of scented flowers in the vivarium, but these should be carefully chosen so that they enhance the appearance of the set-up as well as providing some cover for the frogs. It will also be necessary to add cultured food, in the form of crickets and flies, to the enclosure occasionally.

Breeding among all the European and North American species takes place in spring. With some there is an extended breeding season, lasting into the summer, but others breed only once. Often the whole population will spawn within a day or two of each other. Each female lays several hundred – sometimes over 1000 – eggs in a large, gelatinous mass. They float on or beneath the surface and are easily seen. At this point a decision must be made as to how many young can be reared: if it is a local species that is being kept it may be convenient to remove 90 per cent or so of the eggs and place them in a neighbouring pond. This is feasible only if the populations are the same, however: French spawn should never be released into a British pond, for instance, even if the species is found there. Alternatively, the surplus spawn can be distributed among other enthusiasts and used to seed their garden ponds. Whatever decision is made, there is no doubt that attempting to rear a complete batch of spawn will rarely be successful: the tadpoles will become stunted through lack of space, lack of food, or both, with the end result that only a handful may survive to maturity. It is far better to concentrate on rearing a small number.

If the spawn is left in the pond where it was laid, a number of the tadpoles may get eaten by the adults or by other species if a mixed community is kept. It is worth repeating that newts are voracious predators on frog tadpoles and one or two pairs of co-habiting newts will often polish off a complete spawning in a matter of a few weeks.

When the young metamorphose, towards the end of summer in most cases, they will disperse throughout the enclosure and find food for themselves. As they are more agile than the adults, they may well disperse throughout the garden and neighbouring gardens, so pre-cautions must be taken if this is considered undesirable. Tadpoles which have been reared separately, either in aquaria or in another pond, can either by returned to the main enclosure once they have metamorphosed or they can be placed in a separate rearing enclosure, perhaps a coldframe.

In areas where winters vary in their severity, it may be a good idea to remove a proportion of the adults and/or young frogs during the autumn and house them in a safer place, perhaps a frost-free greenhouse or a cool room indoors. They should not require feeding provided they are cool, and may be conveniently stored in plastic food containers packed with moist sphagnum moss.

European common frog, *Rana temporaria*

Easily the most familiar frog to European readers, *Rana temporaria* is brown, yellow or greenish in colour with a distinctive black 'mask' around the eyes. It is not as aquatic as several of the other species and will live happily for most of the year in damp grass, beneath logs and so on without access to water. It does require a pool to breed in, of course, and so the type of enclosure outlined above is equally suitable for this species as well as the more aquatic ones.

189

Breeding takes place explosively, very early in the spring when the temperature is not much above freezing point. Unless their breeding activities are interrupted by a very cold spell, all females will spawn within a week of each other, or less.

SIMILAR SPECIES

Rana sylvatica, the North American wood frog, is almost identical to *R. temporaria*. Although it not widely kept, it can be assumed that its care and life-history are as above.

Edible frog, *Rana esculenta*

The edible frog is an altogether more colourful species than the common frog and grows slightly larger, with a maximum size of about 12 cm. Its back may be brown, green or beige and there is often a pale, broad, vertical stripe. The vocal sacs are paired. This species is very aquatic, rarely straying more than a few centimetres from the water's edge. It likes to bask in the sun and the enclosure should not be situated in too shady a spot.

Breeding in this species is delayed until the water has begun to warm up. Although it may be active early in the year, the first spawn will not appear until late spring or early summer. Breeding activity continues until midsummer.

American bullfrog, *Rana catesbeiana*

The American bullfrog is rarely offered for sale in its adult form, but its tadpoles are often available, usually through tropical fish dealers. In addition an albino strain is sometimes obtainable. The tadpoles should be treated like other frog tadpoles: that is, kept in clean, matured water and fed on fish flake. Larger tadpoles will also take whiteworm and other freeze-dried fish foods. The real problems begin at metamorphosis! Bullfrogs grow to an enormous size, potentially to 20 cm, and require huge, semi-aquatic vivaria, heated to about 20°C. In addition to insects, the adults will eat small mice. They will also devour any other small amphibians that come their way, and so they must be kept separately. Although some individuals 'tame down' reasonably well, most are nervous and leap into the water at the slightest disturbance. Captive breeding has been achieved only through hormone induction, and then only under laboratory conditions. In all honesty, these frogs have little to recommend them as long-term captives except to dedicated specialists.

89.   Tadpole of the American bullfrog. These are frequently sold at tropical fish outlets and make interesting captives – for a while!

90.   American bullfrog, *Rana catesbeiana*. Adults of this species can be difficult to accommodate satisfactorily unless space is unlimited.

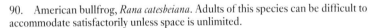

191

Leopard frogs, *Rana pipiens* complex

The North American leopard frogs have a collective range from southern Canada, throughout the United States and well into Central America. Although they have been divided into a number of species and subspecies, identification is not simple unless locality data is available (and it usually isn't). Since their care and, in particular, their suitability for housing in outside enclosures are dependent on their place of origin, this can present something of a problem. In my experience these species make rather poor captives, perhaps as a result of the above factors. Although they have been extensively bred in laboratories, this has invariably been as a result of hormone-induced spawning.

SIMILAR SPECIES

Over the years numerous species of *Rana* have been imported and offered for sale. Temperate species from Europe and North America can be treated as above, but the tropical and subtropical species require much more warmth and are suitable for keeping only in heated indoor vivaria. Although they are interesting, their frenetic activities, often resulting in injuries to their snouts, make keeping them less of a pleasure than keeping many other frogs and toads.

2: AFRICAN BULLFROG

The African bullfrog, *Pyxicephalus adspersus*, is the African equivalent of the South American horned frogs: huge, inactive and blessed with a cavernous mouth. Juveniles are spotted, vary from brown to green in colour and have a light, vertebral stripe which starts on their snout. As they grow, the spots and the stripe become less distinct until the adult animals, occasionally reaching 20 cm in length, are plain olive-green on the back, yellow on the flanks and dirty white beneath. The hind-legs have a blade-like tubercle which acts as a spade when the frog burrows backwards into the soil.

This species is not difficult to keep in captivity. Its requirements are similar to those of the *Ceratophrys* species which it parallels, and it can also be kept in a vivarium furnished with a 10 cm layer of peat and sphagnum moss on the bottom which should be kept reasonably moist but not soggy. It will eat just about anything which fits into its mouth – large insects, small rodents and other frogs. Young specimens are highly cannibalistic and should not be housed together.

91. African bullfrog, *Pyxicephalus adspersus*. A large and voracious species which is easily accommodated.

In nature this species breeds after a long, dry period, during which time it burrows down into the mud and forms a cocoon of shed skins around its body to reduce water loss. Heavy rain, which floods the surrounding countryside, is the cue for mating activity and males take up territories around the shallow edges of the temporary pools. In captivity, breeding has thus far been achieved only by the use of hormones, but it seems reasonable to assume that if the frogs are dried and cooled for a time, then placed in warm, shallow water, it should be possible to induce spawning naturally. Rearing the tadpoles is straight-forward, but when they begin to metamorphose each one should be housed separately otherwise they will decimate one another.

3: MANTELLAS

The genus *Mantella* is restricted to Madagascar. As with the South American poison-dart frogs, to which the members of the genus bear a close superficial resemblance, their taxonomy is in a state of flux; several new species have been described recently, although some of these are almost certainly just colour variants of one another. There

193

appear to be five or six good species, several of which occur in various forms, making identification sometimes difficult. It is to be hoped that a more authoritative revision will be available soon to make life easier for mantella fanciers!

All mantellas are small, active frogs from the rapidly shrinking rainforest areas of Madagascar, where they live on the ground among fallen leaves. They are imported spasmodically, but several species are regularly bred in captivity.

Mantellas prefer rather cooler conditions than the dendrobatids, ideally about 20°C and with a maximum of 25°C. They are very resistant to cold and, in a moderately heated house, require very little supplementary heating. During winter they will become less active and will require only occasional feeding. In spring their appetites will increase and they should be fed well in preparation for the breeding season. Food consists of small insects such as hatchling crickets, fruit flies and small waxworms. Each meal should be liberally dusted with a vitamin and mineral supplement, especially if breeding is anticipated.

Small groups of these frogs may be simply kept in a small vivarium with a layer of leaf-litter on the floor, a few pieces of bark and the odd potted plant. Although they have rather specialized breeding habits, elaborate set-ups are not always essential. Many breeders favour a cage with a large water area, 4-5 cm deep. This can be gently circulated if necessary. Peat blocks or chunks of tree fern root should be placed in the water in such a way that there are dark caves and crevices above the surface. The land area may be filled with leaf-litter or it too can consist of peat blocks and tree fern root. These conditions, apart from suiting the frogs, are ideal for growing epiphytic orchids, ferns and mosses, and it is not difficult to create an attractive display in which the animals will feel at home.

Prior to breeding, feeding should be intensified. The females will begin to swell with eggs and it is only at this time that the sexes can be distinguished easily. Males begin to call when conditions are right for breeding. If a female is ready to mate, she will approach a male and they will disappear together into one of the caves in order to spawn. The eggs, numbering twenty or more depending on age and species, are laid on a damp substrate – that is, the peat blocks or tree fern root – just above the water level. When they hatch, about ten days later, the tadpoles slide down into the shallow water and continue to develop in the normal way. These frogs will also breed without the aquatic facilities described: the eggs are then laid on moss and, before they hatch, they should be removed to a container with a few millimetres of conditioned water.

Newly hatched tadpoles should be handled carefully with a small net or tea-strainer and reared in shallow water in a small aquarium or plastic food container. A handful of Java moss can be placed in the water and the tadpoles will feed on this or on algae. Additional food can be given in the form of fish flake of the kind produced for herbivorous fish. Metamorphosis will begin in about four weeks and the water level should be lowered at this time to prevent the small frogs from drowning. When they begin to emerge, the container should be tilted to allow them easy access to dry land.

The newly metamorphosed froglets are minute and require a constant supply of springtails at first. As they grow they will graduate to fruit flies and then slightly larger insects. It takes about one year for the juveniles to reach breeding size.

Golden mantella, *Mantella aurantiaca*

The golden mantella is probably the most familiar species. It grows to about 2.5 cm in length and is uniform bright orange in colour. There is some variation in the shade of orange, however, some individuals tending towards yellow and others tending towards reddish-orange.

92. Golden mantella, *Mantella aurantiaca*, one of the most beautiful of Madagascar's interesting selection of frogs and toads.

This mantella was the first of its genus to breed in captivity and is among the hardiest. Its care and breeding are as outlined above. An alternative arrangement, which has proved reasonably successful, is to keep the frogs in a large, heavily planted rainforest-type vivarium with running water. Provided suitable sites are available, the eggs will be hidden and can be left to hatch and develop without further attention. The froglets will disperse throughout the vivarium and at least some of them will find sufficient food to thrive, so the colony will be self-perpetuating.

Mantella crocea

Mantella crocea is among the smallest species of mantellas. It is rather dull in coloration, compared to the others, being mainly bronze-brown with a solid black area extending from the snout, over the eyes and on to each flank. Its care and breeding are as described above.

93. *Mantella madagascariensis*. This species occurs in a number of forms and is frequently listed as *Mantella 'cowani'*.

94. *Mantella viridis*. Another species that occurs in a number of colour phases: this is one of the more attractive ones.

Mantella madagascariensis

Mantella madagascariensis is now considered to include the forms previously described as *M. cowani* and *M. pulchra*. This is a beautiful and intricately marked species with several variations. It grows to about 2.5 cm. The top of the head and the centre of the back are glossy black. The fore-limbs are bright canary-yellow or lime-green and there are stripes of a similar colour extending from the snout, over each eye and on to the flanks. The hind-limbs may be yellow or orange or both, with or without bars of black. Some forms have blue markings on the throat and at the base of the fore-limbs.

This appears to be an accommodating species which breeds fairly regularly in captivity using the methods described above.

Mantella viridis

Despite its specific name, *Mantella viridis* is not green. The most frequently seen form is bronze above, becoming darker on the back,

197

with metallic-blue patches around the bases of the fore-limbs and hind-limbs. There is a bright red area on the inside of the hind-limbs. Other colour forms have been described.

This species is infrequently seen and there is little information on its care and breeding. It is assumed to have similar requirements to the others listed.

SIMILAR SPECIES

Apart from the species and synonyms listed, there are apparently two other species: *Mantella betsileo* and *M. laevigata*. Due to problems with identification it is difficult to know whether these are in circulation.

CHAPTER 24

Hyperoliidae: Reed Frogs, Bush Frogs and Related Species

The family Hyperoliidae, numbering about 300 species in all, is restricted to Africa, Madagascar and the Seychelles. Most species are small, arboreal frogs which inhabit the margins of ponds, lakes and swamps. Those in the genus *Leptopelis*, however, are sometimes found in drier situations and may burrow to escape desiccation at certain times of the year. Typical species have adhesive toe-pads with which they climb, although these are reduced in size in the less arboreal types. Unfortunately only a small proportion of the species, mainly those belonging to the genus *Hyperolius*, are available.

These species, and probably others as well, are easily maintained in small-to-medium-sized vivaria with a large area of water. Semi-aquatic plants can be placed in the water, but the frogs will invariably perch in the corners of the cage, usually just under the top. They are active mainly at night. A temperature of 20-25°C should be maintained throughout the year, and a diet of crickets and, especially, flying insects is suitable; these should be dusted with vitamin and mineral powder.

Marbled reed frog, *Hyperolius marmoratus*

The southern African species *Hyperolius marmoratus* is one of the most common and occurs in a bewildering variety of colours and markings. Even from the same population, individuals may be boldly striped in cream and brown, spotted or marbled with the same combination of colours, or plain brown. The underside is invariably pale cream to white and the thighs and feet are pink. It grows to a little over 2.5 cm in length.

Breeding appears to take place with little or no stimulation, although spraying the cage regularly with water may help to induce mating behaviour. Specimens collected from the wild may breed only during the northern winter (that is, spring and summer in their natural range) but captive-bred animals can spawn at any time of the year. Males start to vocalize in the early evening: their call is rather like the noise produced by a squeaky wheelbarrow. Spawning invariably takes place at night.

A successful way of breeding this species is to place a handful of Java moss in the water area, which should be about 10 cm deep. The females attach their spawn, consisting of about ten clumps each containing twenty eggs, to the moss, which can then be removed to a rearing aquarium. If the moss is replaced each time spawn is found, there will always be fresh substrate for subsequent eggs. If the adults are well fed, repeated spawnings take place every ten to fourteen days for about three months of the year.

The tadpoles can be reared in a plastic food container. The eggs hatch in about three days: gentle aeration of the water seems to improve the hatch rate, which is often 100 per cent. The tadpoles are fed on fish flake and metamorphose about two months later. The young froglets are relatively large and will eat small crickets, fruit flies and similar items, all of which should be well dusted with a vitamin and mineral powder. The juveniles are pale brown, the adult coloration only appearing when they approach reproductive size about six months later.

Hyperolius viridiflavus

Hyperolius viridiflavus, a Kenyan species, grows to 2.5 cm in length and is uniform green above, and yellow beneath. Its feet are pinkish.

In captivity it requires similar conditions to those described for *H. marmoratus*. It will spawn in small dishes, however, and is less seasonal: females can produce clutches of 200-400 eggs every two to three weeks throughout the year if conditions are suitable. Obviously, intensive breeding such as this is not possible without an equally intensive feeding regime.

SIMILAR SPECIES

Numerous species of *Hyperolius* are found throughout southern and East Africa. Although they rarely find their way into the pet trade, they are all potentially good vivarium subjects. Little is known about the care and breeding of most of these species, but the methods used for *H. marmoratus* would seem to be a good starting point. A few species, however, such as *H. tuberilinguis* and *H. pusillus*, lay their eggs out of water, attached to emergent vegetation. These would require a rather

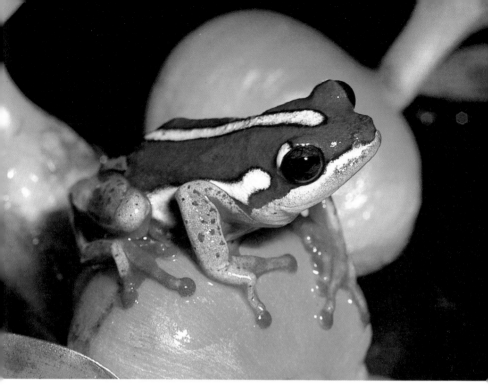

95. An unidentified reed frog, *Hyperolius* species. Many of these small African frogs are brightly marked and thrive in a semi-aquatic environment. Some have bred in captivity.

different arrangement and some experimentation may be necessary before the correct conditions could be met.

The species belonging to the closely related *Afrixalus* genus differ from *Hyperolius* in having a vertical pupil. In addition they have numerous small, black tubercles on the skin, scattered over the entire body. Their spawning habits are unusual in that the female lays her eggs in small clumps on a leaf, either just above or just below the surface of the water. The male then puts the edges of the leaves together to form a primitive type of nest. In Africa the members of the genus are known as leaf-folding frogs for this reason. They have been bred in captivity but only rarely. They require similar conditions to those described for the *Hyperolius* species.

Striped running frog, *Kassina senegalensis*

Kassina senegalensis is a pretty frog, beige or tan in colour with three prominent black stripes running down its back. It is found in southern and East Africa and is more terrestrial than most of its family, lacking toe-pads altogether. It grows to about 4 cm in length. The male is easily distinguished from the female by his prominent, oval-shaped vocal sac which is obvious even when deflated.

This species requires a vivarium with a covering of slightly moist leaf-litter or potting compost planted with mosses, ferns and grasses. For breeding, a large water area is necessary. A temperature of 20-25°C is required, although a fall in temperature during the night will be tolerated. Food consists of crickets, flies and other small insects. Breeding is induced by raising the humidity of the cage by copious spraying. The male's call is a beautiful fluid 'whoop', uttered repeatedly. Successful spawning is something of a rare event in captivity, but females apparently lay up to 400 eggs attached to water plants. The tadpoles eat algae and also small aquatic invertebrates, such as white-worms and mosquito larvae. They take about three months to reach metamorphosis.

SIMILAR SPECIES

The two other members of the genus, *Kassina wealii* and *K. maculata* (sometimes listed as *Hylambates maculata*), are rarely available but can be housed and maintained in the same manner as *K. senegalensis*. There are no records of captive breeding.

The frogs belonging to the genus *Leptopelis* are sometimes known as bush frogs. There are about forty species, several of which have a very small range. They are plumper than other members of the family, not very arboreal, and sometimes burrow to avoid spells of dry weather. Many species are beautifully coloured with bright green in combination with other colours. Little is known of their life-history, although at least one, *L. natalensis*, lays its eggs out of water in damp surroundings. Unfortunately they are not generally available at present and there is little or no information on their care and breeding.

CHAPTER 25

Rhacophoridae: Foam-nest Tree Frogs

Nearly 200 hundred species are placed in the family Rhacophoridae, which consists of mainly arboreal frogs from Africa and South-east Asia. The majority of species, including all the well-known ones, lay their eggs in balls of foam that they whip up with their hind-limbs during the spawning process.

These frogs parallel the American and Eurasian hylids, both in appearance and in habits. They have large, expanded toe-pads as an aid to climbing and tend to be most active during the evening and night. A few of the more specialized *Rhacophorus* species have large feet which are heavily webbed: these they use to parachute from high branches to lower ones, or to the ground. Only a relatively small number of species are in general circulation.

African grey tree frog, *Chiromantis xerampelina*

The African grey tree frog grows to about 8 cm in total length. It is grey in colour with only slight traces of darker markings, but in bright light it becomes almost pure white. Males have pale nuptial pads on the first and second fingers of the fore-limbs.

In nature this species experiences temporary droughts and can withstand considerable dehydration. In captivity, however, it should be given a cage with a reasonable degree of humidity, maintained by light spraying, and a substrate of peat or leaf-litter. A temperature of 20-25°C suits it, but if this is allowed to fall slightly no harm will be done. It will eat most insects, but prefers the larger flying varieties, especially moths.

Breeding has apparently occured in captivity, though on only one or two occasions: it is likely that this is because of lack of interest rather than any great difficulties. The suggestions given overleaf are based on the frog's reproductive habits in the wild.

The foam nests are attached to branches overhanging water. In order to breed the species in captivity, therefore, a suitable arrangement would have to be constructed in the vivarium. Breeding in the wild is stimulated by the onset of heavy rains, so it should be possible to induce it by first allowing the cage to become progressively drier: this causes the frogs to cling tightly to branches or to the sides of the vivarium in order to conserve water. After two or three weeks the cage should be thoroughly sprayed every day until the water area is filled. Males will normally start calling soon after spraying commences, and, if all goes well, spawning will take place subsequently. The tadpoles hatch from the foam nest and drip into the water. They are herbivorous and rearing should therefore be straightforward.

SIMILAR SPECIES

There are two other species in the genus, *Chiromantis petersii* and *C. rufescens*. Their habits in the wild are similar to those of *C. xerampelina*, and suggestions for breeding that species may also be tried with these.

Asian tree frog, *Polypedates leucomystax*

A common species, formerly known as *Rhacophorus leucomystax*, the Asian tree frog occurs in a variety of habitats in South-east Asia and even breeds in the centre of cities. Its foam nest may be attached to branches, to the banks of streams or pools or to the sides (often in the corners) of man-made concrete wells and cisterns. Females may grow to almost 10 cm, but males are considerably smaller. It is variable in colour and individuals may change colour in response to light levels and mood. At one extreme they may be pale brown or creamy-brown, at the other they can be dark chocolate-brown or reddish-brown. All intermediate shades are possible. In the pale phase there may or may not be darker stripes on the jaws, hind-legs and dorsum.

Maintaining this species is quite straightforward. The frogs require tall, roomy vivaria thickly planted with tropical plants such as *Philodendron* and other house plant species. If breeding is anticipated, some of these plants should overhang an aquatic area comprising about one third of the floor space. Tropical temperatures, within the range 25-30°C are necessary and all the usual insect fare will be accepted, especially flies and other flying insects.

Spawning follows a period of heavy spraying on a daily or twice-daily regime. It may be helpful to reduce the humidity for a week or two prior to this, although it is by no means certain that it is essential. The eggs are deposited in a ball of foam, whipped up by the hind-legs of

96.   Asian tree frog, *Polypedates leucomystax*, a common foam-nest species which adapts readily to captivity (see also photograph 25).

the female, and usually attached to the sides of the vivarium rather than to the plants. They will normally be placed in such a way that the tadpoles drop into the water when they hatch four or five days later. At this point the tadpoles should be removed from the vivarium and reared in a separate aquarium. They are herbivorous and can be reared in the normal way. The largest will begin to metamorphose after about one month and the remainder will follow over an extended period of time.

Rhacophorus species

A number of *Rhacophorus* species have been available, off and on, usually in small numbers. Some of these, such as *R. reinwardtii*, *R. nigropalmatus* and so on, are among the species popularly known as

205

97. One of the Asian 'flying' frogs, *Rhacophorus nigropalmatus*. These large tree frogs make spectacular exhibits but require very large cages.

'flying frogs': they have heavily webbed hands and feet and flaps of skin on their legs which they use to 'parachute' from tall trees and shrubs. All species are active and agile, however, and require large vivaria, ideally 1 m in height or more. These should be heavily planted and furnished with plenty of stout vertical and horizontal branches on which the frogs can perch. A temperature of 25-30°C should be maintained at all times, as should a high humidity. A set-up with running water would be especially suitable. Food consists of invertebrates, especially flying insects.

All species build foam nests, but the requirements necessary to induce them to breed in captivity are unknown through lack of a regular supply of stock.

CHAPTER 26

Microhylidae: Narrow-mouthed Frogs

The Microhylidae has an almost worldwide distribution and contains nearly 300 species. Many of these are small, nondescript burrowing frogs in which there is little interest, but a few species are large and rather more colourful. Some are kept and bred in captivity.

Typical microhylids are rotund in shape and burrowing in habit. Some, such as the African rain frogs, *Breviceps*, are almost exclusively subterranean, even to the point of breeding in underground chambers, and these present obvious problems when it comes to care and breeding. Others burrow to avoid drought and are more terrestrial under favourable conditions, and these can make interesting captives. The few arboreal species, from Madagascar, are largely unknown at present.

Tomato frog, *Discophus antongilli*

The tomato frog and one or two other members of its genus are relatively new arrivals as far as amateur herpetoculturalists are concerned. They originate from Madagascar and are unarguably the most colourful microhylids. Healthy specimens are blood-red in colour without markings. Males are considerably smaller than females and this is the best way to tell the sexes apart.

These frogs are terrestrial and should be kept on a deep layer of leaf-litter or peaty soil. They are secretive and should be given plenty of hiding places. Since they burrow, plants in the vivaria should be left in their pots and plunged into the substrate. Water may be provided in a shallow bowl or tray. The frogs do not appear to be particular regarding temperature: although they are normally kept at 25-30°C, they will come to no harm if the temperature is allowed to fall (gradually) to 15-20°C occasionally. They accept all the usual insect fare, which should be dusted with a vitamin and mineral supplement at every feeding.

Although most breeding successes have been as a result of hormone inducement, the frogs have occasionally bred naturally. This has been achieved by conditioning the animals well, allowing the humidity to fall for about one month and then spraying them heavily. Alternatively they can be placed in a 'rain chamber' (see Chapter 7). About 1000 floating eggs are laid at a time. These hatch after two days and the tadpoles can be reared on fish flake. Metamorphosis starts to take place after six weeks, but will continue for several more weeks before all the froglets have emerged. At this stage they are unable to swim well and may easily drown if they are not helped out of the water by the provision of a sloping layer of gravel or foam rubber. The tiny froglets are not red but brown, the adult coloration coming through gradually by the time they are about three months old. They can be set up in the same manner as the adults and fed on the smallest grade of crickets or sweepings. They grow quite quickly and may reach sexual maturity within one year.

SIMILAR SPECIES

The genus *Discophus* contains several other species, some of which are rarely seen. All the species which have been imported over the last few years appear to adapt to captivity as readily as *D. antongilli* and their requirements are similar.

Gastrophryne species

The two North American *Gastrophryne* species, *G. olivacea* and *G. carolinensis*, are known as narrow-mouthed frogs. They grow to about 3 cm and are plump, with short limbs and a pointed snout. There is a characteristic fold of skin immediately behind the head. Both species are grey or greyish-green in colour, with a faint scattering of small, black dots over the back. *G. carolinensis* has pale flanks and a pigmented underside, whereas *G. olivacea* has a plain dorsum and is dirty white beneath. They are secretive in their habits and are usually found beneath logs and stones.

Both species do well in captivity in the most basic of set-ups, although there are no records of captive breeding. All they require is a small vivarium with a layer of leaf-litter covering the bottom. A few pieces of bark or some flat rocks will provide suitable hiding places, and they will burrow down and form chambers beneath these. They eat any small insects, such as young crickets, waxworms and graded sweepings.

There seem to have been few attempts to breed these little frogs in

98. Narrow-mouthed toad, *Gastrophryne olivacea*, a small North American species which would repay further attention from frog keepers.

captivity. It would seem to be a simple matter to keep them cool during winter, then warm them up in spring, at the same time spraying the cage heavily and providing a small pool in which they could spawn. The male's call has been likened to the bleating of sheep!

Asian bullfrog or painted frog, *Kaloula pulchra*

Kaloula pulchra is frequently imported from South-east Asia. The female grows to 8 cm in length; the male is rather smaller, rarely exceeding 6 cm. The basic colour is dark greyish-brown or olive-brown and there are two broad tan or beige stripes running across the top of the head and along each flank. The male can be identified by his darker throat. As with many members of the family, the snout is blunt.

This is a tropical species which should be kept at 25-30°C. It requires a layer of leaf-litter or peaty soil, with pieces of wood under

99.   Asian bullfrog or painted frog, *Kaloula pulchra*, one of the larger microhylids and an interesting exhibit.

which to hide. Plants should be left in their pots to avoid disturbance of their roots. The frogs will eat the usual insect fare, selected according to their size.

In the wild, breeding is stimulated by heavy rain (the monsoon) following a period of drought. This can be simulated in captivity by allowing the vivarium to dry out slightly for a few weeks, then spraying it heavily. At the same time a large water container should be installed or, better still, an aquatic area can be allowed to flood. The males call from shallow water: the call can best be described as suggestive of a cow in pain.

The eggs float, hatch quickly and can be reared in the usual way. Development is rapid and the first froglets may begin to metamorphose in less than one month. They can be fed on small crickets and other insects, dusted with a vitamin and mineral preparation.

Microhyla species

Frogs belonging to the genus *Microhyla* are imported occasionally. There are several common species, any of which may be present in shipments from South-east Asia. They are small-to-medium-sized frogs of secretive life-style which breed in temporary puddles of water during the rainy season. They appear not to have been bred in captivity, probably because of lack of interest rather than any great difficulty, and it is safe to assume that they could be encouraged to spawn in much the same way as the Asian bullfrog or the tomato frog.

Banded rubber frog, *Phrynomerus bifasciatus*

The amazing little banded rubber frog is one of the African representatives of the family, although it and the other three members of the genus are sometimes placed in a family of their own.

Growing to about 5 cm in length, it is shiny black in colour with two broad pink or red stripes down either side of its back and spots of a similar colour on its limbs. In short, it looks like a large, wet licorice sweet!

100. Banded rubber frog, *Phrynpmerus bifasciatus*, an unusual African microhylid which has rather specialized requirements.

Unfortunately, it does not make a particularly good captive. It is secretive and nervous, spending most of its time buried. It requires a similar set-up to that described for *Kaloula pulchra*, for instance, but is more tolerant of cool temperatures. It prefers small prey items, which should be plentiful. Captive breeding has not been achieved with any degree of regularity. As with the other species listed, it breeds in response to heavy rains after a dry spell, and this should be simulated in the vivarium. Unlike the other species, however, it lays its eggs out of water in damp vegetation, from which the tadpoles wriggle into the water when they hatch ten to fourteen days later. They metamorphose after about eight weeks and the small froglets require plenty of small insects such as springtails, aphids and fruit flies.

Specialist societies, journals and magazines

Unfortunately, addresses of contacts are likely to change throughout the life of this book and so cannot usefully be included. Most societies cater for reptiles as well as amphibians.

American Federation of Herpetoculturalists, Lakeside, California 92040, USA.
Publication: *Vivarium*. Six issues per year. Also available through reptile and amphibian dealers.

Australasian Federation of Herpetological Societies, Sydney, Australia.
Publication: *Herpetofauna*. Four issues per year.

British Dendrobatid Group, Ayr, Scotland.
Publication: *BDG Newsletter*. Issued monthly.

British Herpetological Society, London, England.
Publication: *Bulletin of the British Herpetological Society*. Four issues per year.

Dendrobatidae Nederland, Rijssen, Netherlands.
Publication: *Dendrobatidae Magazine* (Dutch and English editions).

Deutschen Gesellschaft fur Herpetologie und Terrarienkunde, Frankfurt, Germany.
Publication: *Salamandra* (in German). Four issues per year.

Herpetofauna Verlags, Weinstadt, Germany.
Publication: *Herpetofauna* (in German). Four issues per year.

International Herpetological Society, Walsall, West Midlands, England.
Publication: *The Herptile*. Four issues per year.

International Society for the Study of Dendrobatids, Arizona, USA.
Publication: *ISSD Newsletter.*

Nederlandse Vereniging voor Herpetologie en Terrarienkunde,
Amsterdam, Netherlands.
Publication: *Lacerta* (in Dutch). Six issues per year.

Reptile and Amphibian Magazine. Pottsville, Pennsylvania, USA.
Bi-monthly.
Available through reptile and amphibian dealers.

Bibliography

Books and important articles

The journals and newsletters listed on pages 213–14 are the richest sources of information on keeping and breeding amphibians. Additional important material is listed here, although much of it may be difficult to obtain.

Blatchford, Dave. 'Environmental Lighting', *Proceedings of the 1986 UK Herpetological Societies Symposium on Captive Breeding*, 87-97.

British Herpetological Society. *Establishing and Maintaining Crested Newts in Garden Ponds* (4 pages, London, 1983).

British Herpetological Society. *Garden Ponds as Amphibian Sanctuaries* (4 pages, London, 1984).

de Vosjoli, Phillippe. *The General Care and Maintenance of White's Tree Frogs* (Advance Vivarium Systems, Lakeside, California, 1990).

de Vosjoli, Phillippe. *The General Care and Maintenance of Horned Frogs* (Advance Vivarium Systems, Lakeside, California, 1990).

Duellman, W.E., and Trueb, L. *Biology of Amphibians* (McGraw-Hill Book Company, New York, 1985).

Heselhaus, Ralf. *Poison-Arrow Frogs* (Blandford Press, London 1992).

Johnson, Robert. 'Breeding the Bell's Horned Frog (*Ceratophrys ornata*): an alternative to hormonally induced reproduction', *Proceedings of the 8th Annual International Symposium on Captive Propagation and Husbandry*, 22-32 (Columbus, Ohio, 1984).

McClain, J.M., Odum, R.A., and Shely, T.C. 'Hormonally induced breeding and rearing of White's tree frog (*Litoria caerulea*)', *Proceedings of the 7th Annual International Symposium on Captive Propagation and Husbandry*, 34-9 (Columbus, Ohio, 1983).

Nace, George W. 'The Amphibian Facility of the University of Michigan', *Bioscience*, Vol. 18 (8), 767-75.

Odum, Andrew. 'Water quality, an often overlooked parameter for the amphibian enclosure', *Proceedings of the 8th Annual International Symposium on Captive Propagation and Husbandry*, 33-58, (Columbus, Ohio, 1984).

Sterba, G. *Aquarium Care* (Studio Vista, London, 1967).

Yearbooks and symposium reports

In recent years various societies have held symposia on keeping and breeding reptiles and amphibians. Published reports are usually available through the relevant societies.

International Zoo Yearbook. Published annually by the Zoological Society of London. This publication often contains articles on the care and breeding of amphibians along with other zoo-related material.

Reports of the International Herpetological Symposium on Captive Propagation and Husbandry. Published reports of the annual symposia held at various locations in the USA from 1976 onwards.

Index

Page references in *italics* refer to illustrations.